HOW TO MAKE POWERFUL SPEECHES

HOW TO MAKE POWERFUL SPEECHES:

A Step-by-Step Guide to Inspiring and Memorable Speeches

Eamonn O'Brien

ISBN 978-0-9928164-5-2

Published in 2014, 2015 by The Reluctant Speakers Club

64 Lower Mount Street
Dublin 2, Ireland

www.thereluctantspeakersclub.com

For permission or bulk purchase inquiries, please email **publishing@thersc.ie**

To Mindy, Conor and Meg

IN GRATITUDE

Sometimes chance can play a role in shaping what we do during our lives. And I know my passion for public speaking would never have been piqued in the same way were it not for an elective course I happened to choose while spending a semester at the Kellogg School of Management MBA programme in the early 1990s.

The late and hugely inspiring Professor Marty Stoller ran a course called Business Communication. And if I'm honest, I signed up for his course more because it sounded fascinating than any thoughts about whether or how it might stretch me. The promise he made for his programme was that it would help participants to uncover what it takes to be a more effective and engaging communicator. And did it ever deliver. In those 12 weeks I was introduced to the ancient topic of rhetoric – the art of persuading others through your words – and I was hooked. I was struck by how this ancient and essential subject, which sadly is rarely taught or promoted in schools or colleges around the world today, should be a core part of every businessperson's education. After all, this science offers the possibility of making most every form of business and personal communication more engaging, memorable and persuasive. Thank you Marty for opening my eyes to the wisdom of Aristotle, Cicero, Plato and other ancient communication sages from whom we should all learn so much. I owe you a greater debt than I can ever articulate.

My thanks also go to the plethora of people who encouraged me and helped me to write this book. To my copy editor Antoinette Walker, who helped to transform me from a writer of blogs to a writer of books; to my trusted advisors and mentors Noel Derby, Ivan Walsh, Amanda Webb, Bob Bly and Krishna De who helped to steer what I shared with you in this book, and to my wonderful book designer Alan McDonnell who transforms words into a reading experience through his graphical magic – I am so grateful to you, one and all.

Finally, this book would never have come into being without the unceasing support of my wife Mindy and my children Conor and Meg. Thank you for buoying me up and cheering me on through the long and sometimes lonely journey of writing a book. It has been a blast and I love you all.

CONTENTS

PART 1
WHY YOU NEED TO DEVELOP PUBLIC SPEAKING SKILLS   18

Why Learning to Speak in Public Matters   18

PART 2
THE FOUNDATIONS YOU NEED TO
BE A PERSUASIVE SPEAKER   25

How Ancient Secrets Can Make You More Persuasive   25

Speech Building Blocks: Audience Analysis 33

Speech Building Blocks: Relevance   42

Speech Building Blocks: Credibility   48

PART 3
THE FOCUS AND STRUCTURE OF A COMPELLING SPEECH 57

How to Construct a Compelling Speech   57

Developing Content   75

Creating Engagement, Insights and Memories   92

Using PowerPoint and Other Visual Aids   110

Handling Questions and Comments   126

PART 4
HONING YOUR SPEECH VIA DELIVERY

Writing, Honing and Owning Your Speech   137

CONTENTS

Last Minute Checks 214

Dealing with the Unexpected 221

INTRODUCTION

Picture the scene. A large crowd has assembled and is mostly settled. There's a hush as the master of ceremonies prepares to make your introduction. You're about to step out in front of all these people and speak.

- What's going through your mind?
- Are the butterflies in your stomach 'flying in formation'?
- Are you dreading what is to follow or excited to get started?

Just imagine knowing how to address any audience, no matter how large or important, with no fear and no trace of overconfidence as you share messages that inspire others into action.

I can still remember the early 1990s when I was asked to speak in front of my first mega crowd in a telecom PLC in the USA. I use the term 'asked' very loosely you understand, the actual conversation went roughly like this:

Boss: 'Great news. I got you a spot at the "All Hands" in Phoenix.'

Me: 'Sounds good. What's that and who'll be there?'

Boss: 'Oh, it's an annual strategy session for all our senior people. Should be maybe 700 to 800 there – you know, the usual suspects: directors, VPs and most of the senior managers. They'll love you and your Irish brogue.'

At this point, the penny dropped and I was stunned...

Me: 'So ... when you mentioned a spot for me, you meant a spot as in the standing-up-and-talking-to-the-crowd variety?'

Boss: 'Of course. It's a great chance for you to tell everyone all about that ethnic marketing stuff you know so much about. Go and drum up more support for your advertising campaigns.'

Now I was speechless.

Boss: 'Oh, and one more thing... You'll be on just before the CEO speaks, so make sure you don't let the side down, OK?'

No pressure then!

But I didn't crumble, and the reason was simple. During the previous year I had been fortunate enough to learn some essential public speaking skills from a most inspirational man, the late Professor Marty Stoller at the Kellogg School of Management at Northwestern University. I set about figuring out how to apply and adapt my learning to make it work at such an important event. I also put in the hard work to prepare myself, practising like blazes long before I got anywhere near that podium.

On the day, my talk was low on detail and big on 'show don't tell' examples of why speaking to an audience in their own language could make a difference. I included a story about Eva, an 84-year-old Russian woman and Auschwitz survivor, who had become so talked about in MCI's call centres. Anna, her 60-year-old daughter, had rung one of our call centres in a highly agitated state.

'My mother is going to die if I can't sign her up for your cheap calls to Russia, right now,' she said.

You might think that this woman was exaggerating. She wasn't. It turned out that her mother Eva had a heart attack and needed immediate surgery. But she was refusing to have this vital job done. And all for a phone deal! She was going nowhere until she could hear from her daughter that she had qualified for cheap calls to her one remaining sister back in

Russia. She was willing to risk life and limb for an emotional connection with a loved one.

As I told this and other stories, I could see my audience visibly becoming more and more engaged. And as they became more relaxed, so did I. Gone were any fears I may have had about things that might go wrong – I just enjoyed being with the audience and bringing to life messages that could inspire action after I sat down.

When I finished speaking I was delighted to be treated to rapturous applause, beaming smiles, hollers and even a stray wolf whistle. But if I was elated by the reaction of the audience, I was even more boosted by what happened next. Directly after me, the CEO started her address with the words:

'So, great ... who decided to put me on after Conan O'Brien's Irish cousin? How the hell do I follow that?'

Did I feel great? You bet! But it turned out that this was only the start. That one speech gave me instant companywide credibility. I was now recognised as a 'go to' person and expert on cross-cultural marketing. This was then followed in short order by request after request for me to speak at company and external events all over America. This singular set of skills had done more to boost my visibility and personal brand in less than 20 minutes than I could have achieved otherwise in the normal course of events.

Were it not for a quirk of fate when I met Marty, I would never know how learning to speak well in public could really boost both a person and their career. I didn't just learn to speak in public, I discovered skills that allowed me to truly engage audiences, and I learned to conquer fear with confidence. Since then, I have had the privilege of being able to apply and add to these skills both as a speaker and as a coach, in many industries, continents and situations spanning more than twenty years.

Through this book, I look forward to sharing many tools, techniques and approaches I've already shared with thousands of clients at The Reluctant Speakers Club. Now you too can learn the art of persuasive public speaking, and these skills have never been more important.

Everyone in business with a level of responsibility and authority relies on the spoken word to communicate messages and get things done. Whatever audience you would like to influence, this step-by-step guide will help you to speak in public with a greater degree of clarity, persuasiveness and confidence. It can help you to banish your fears of the podium.

Whether you are a new or experienced speaker, you will learn how to connect with an audience, construct arguments, and give talks for maximum impact and persuasion. If you need to regularly, or even occasionally, stand in front of others and inspire them through your words, this book is for you.

WHAT'S IN THE BOOK?

If you follow the steps in this book, you'll gain the tools to consistently create and deliver more engaging speeches. Part 1 focuses on why you need to develop and hone public speaking skills. Part 2 is about assembling vital foundations. You will discover essential and ancient secrets to set your speeches up for greater impact. You'll learn what it takes to create a persuasive talk and find out what you need before you start to compose a speech. The three building blocks that underpin a speech, namely, audience analysis, relevance and credibility, are also discussed in detail.

In Part 3, you'll find a step-by-step approach to develop a winning structure and to determine what content to include. You'll find practical advice on how you can create engaging and memorable messages. You'll learn how to avoid common speechwriting mistakes and how to make your words stand out, helping you to get your message across in a way that's best for your audience.

In Part 4, you'll learn how to edit and practise your speech so you can deliver it with confidence. You'll find techniques to boost your delivery skills so you can move past fears of speaking and connect with your audience. You'll also learn how to sound and look confident by sharing your message in a style that suits you naturally.

In Part 5, you'll find practical advice to help you bring everything together when the big day comes around. In doing so, you can achieve the results you want from your speech.

And don't forget as a purchaser of this book to register for your FREE RESOURCES at
www.howtomakepowerfulspeeches.com

Here's what is included in your bonus materials:

- A speech writing template you can use to boost the impact of every speech you make

- Articles on how to tackle common speaking problems

- Podcast interviews with world renowned communication experts

- Further public speaking and presentation tips

- And you'll receive free public speaking newsletters

CHAPTER ONE

WHY LEARNING TO SPEAK IN PUBLIC MATTERS

"Be skillful in speech, that you may be strong."

Merikare

The prospect of standing up and speaking in front of an audience is nothing short of terrifying for most adults. If that sounds like you, you really are not alone. Surprisingly large numbers of people feel exactly the same way. In fact, public speaking is consistently voted as the greatest of all human fears – with twice as many people fearing the podium more than death!

According to the National Institute of Mental Health, this fear is so pervasive that 74 per cent of American adults (and the figures are worse elsewhere) admit to some degree of speech anxiety. And the upshot? Far too many people avoid public speaking opportunities, even when they know the difference these could make to getting their ideas noticed.

So what's the problem? Why do people feel this way? The most common answers are fears about all the things that could go wrong and worries about personal consequences. This includes loss of face, feeling foolish and/or being perceived as less credible. Indeed many admit to worrying more about how they 'may' be judged for things that 'might happen' rather than about anything that has actually happened to them before.

INSPIRING OTHERS WITH CONFIDENCE

No matter who you are or what you do, learning to be more persuasive can really boost both the confidence you have in yourself and others place in you. It's little wonder this essential skill is so sought after in every profession, industry and walk of life. In fact, effective communication skills are recognised as more important than anything else to succeed as a senior executive, even ahead of critical thinking, problem solving; collaborative team building and creativity and innovation, according to the American Management Associations Critical Skills Survey in 2012. But being persuasive matters well beyond the boardroom.

If you're the one seeking to persuade, sometimes it's easy, as the people you want to persuade need little or no encouragement. But this may not always be the case. Moreover, if you have to convince many people to do something, you'll often find that you cannot rely on one-on-one conversations to win the day; you may also need to speak with groups.

Regardless, here's some good news. Speaking in front of audiences doesn't have to feel risky. Almost everyone has the capacity to learn what it takes to acquire these essential skills, and here's why it matters...

TRUST – THE NEW IMPERATIVE

Organisation management rules are changing. The ways in which work is organised and executed are rapidly moving away from a reliance on traditional, top-down management hierarchies. The age of new flatter, leaner organisation models that require less formal organisational structures has dawned.

> ## Today's leaders must seek to influence more than control.

Increasingly, decisions are being made by those who do the work rather than those who manage. The trend is towards more work being completed through smaller teams (often including peers from outside their immediate organisation) or on an individual basis. In this environment, modern leaders must now lean more heavily on an ability to persuade and influence than old managerial notions of control. Central to persuading people to do things because they want to is the ability to engender trust.

The modern communicator needs to combine clear and engaging messages with empathy, and a selfless disposition to sway hearts and minds. He or she must answer questions of why, rather than expect blind compliance. They must, above all, earn the confidence of their audience to be persuasive. New and enhanced communication skills are required to lead others in larger organisations today.

Causes that inspire change

In his bestselling book *Tribes: We Need You to Lead Us*, marketing guru **Seth Godin** argues that everyone is not just a marketer or a manager today, most of us have a greater need to lead others too. And while management jobs may be more about 'manipulating resources to get a known job done', becoming a leader requires each of us to 'create changes we believe in'.

In other words, it's about achieving visibility for and traction in 'causes' that inspire others to make changes, to follow and to join in on quests we promote. And more specifically, this requires an ability to create and share 'stories that spread'.

A GAME CHANGER

In this era of social media revolution and information overload, it has become increasingly difficult to get attention from those we wish to persuade. Yet if you need to break through the clutter and get people to notice your ideas or your business, what are you to do?

Seeking opportunities to speak in public can help you to win the visibility you need for your ideas or your business:

1. It can give you **access to undivided attention**.

2. It can get you **seen, heard, remembered and valued**.

3. It can **start conversations** you want to continue later.

Let's look at each of these in turn.

Access to undivided attention

This applies both within your organisation as well as marketing to other organisations. There's an old maxim in marketing – nothing happens if you have the best product in the world and no one knows about you!

Nowadays, almost everyone spends less time consuming traditional media and responds less to direct response marketing. Since 9 out of 10 business decisions now involve online searches, an online presence is required; one that is highly prominent, where your website comes up on the first page of search results. We feel bombarded by 24/7 mobile and web communications, emails and myriad social media sites. For most of us, our attention spans have diminished to ludicrously low levels.

In this context, how can you win and keep the attention of those you want to influence long enough for them to really learn who you are, what you can do or share that is of value, and why they might care? The short answer is that you need to both:

- be where they go when seeking information to make decisions, and
- earn sufficient trust that they are likely to pay attention to you.

Yet it is foolhardy to rely exclusively on online communication to win the day. You need real world communication too. And here's the good news. There is a way to reach your target audience and get exactly the kind of reactions you want, and it's largely free (other than your time) ... enter public speaking.

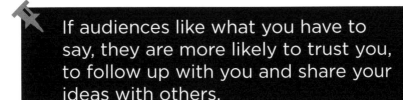

If audiences like what you have to say, they are more likely to trust you, to follow up with you and share your ideas with others.

In the offline world, events are the number one way in which business decision makers gather information from external sources. More than 70 per cent of business executives regularly attend such occasions with their peers and others to network and learn from them. These events include everything from conferences to seminars; information forums to trade shows; networking events to association meetings and more. But what do all of these events have in common?

They're all occasions where anyone who is invited or volunteers to speak will have the opportunity to get undivided access to and attention from those they want to influence. Better still, the organisers of these occasions are almost always crying out for people to give talks, regarding whatever topics they want to address. So if you're a good speaker, chances are you'll be in constant demand.

Be seen, heard, remembered and valued

As long as you speak on topics that provide genuine value to your audiences, public speaking offers you a golden opportunity to demonstrate your knowledge and expertise to your target markets, establishing great credibility for both you and your business. You will find that audiences respond well to those they believe can help them solve problems and make their lives easier.

If they like what you say, they are more likely to trust you; to follow up with you and even to share your ideas with others, through word of mouth. Each of these is an elixir for anyone who wants to get ideas or a business noticed.

Start conversations

Every journey has to start with a first step. Public speaking is a great way to open dialogues with those you want to influence or do business with. Interestingly, it also reassures those who already support your ideas. Used wisely, it can be the difference between whether your ideas are noticed, considered, heeded and actioned, or not.

New and enhanced communication skills are required to lead others in larger organisations today. But before we get into how this applies to you, let's step back in time, to learn how ancient skills can help to set you on a path to more effective communication.

CHAPTER TWO

HOW ANCIENT SECRETS CAN MAKE YOU MORE PERSUASIVE

"Speech is power: Speech is to persuade, to convert, to compel."

Ralph Waldo Emerson

As you begin your journey towards becoming a confident public speaker, it's important not only to develop your skills but also to ground those skills with an understanding of the foundations needed for persuasive communication. Those foundations are built on the art of rhetoric.

THE ART OF RHETORIC

While mankind is constantly focused on progress, especially in the realms of science, technology and health, there are still a few areas where we can learn more from the past than the present. One of these is the art of rhetoric. Rhetoric is really about the art of persuasion through words. It is a collection of skills and philosophies that can help speakers inspire others to believe and/or do things.

Today, the word rhetoric is associated with politicians. Worse, it's commonly used in a derogatory way to describe political claptrap, or the use of words to obscure meaning or repeat the same old ideas again and again by just changing a few words here and there. By that definition, you could be forgiven for thinking that the art of rhetoric might be a bit shady, as if its purpose is to bamboozle, manipulate or even con an audience. Perhaps it even evokes thoughts of a 'snake oil salesman' and his patter, relying on smoke, mirrors and illusions to fool an audience.

While many ancient cultures would have devoted endless energy towards such ideas, it is the Greeks who are historically given the credit for first writing about the topic, and moulding it into a body of teaching or philosophies. The first known teacher of rhetoric was a Greek called Corax.

The story of Corax and Tisias

Corax had a spot of bother with a student named Tisias in the fifth century BC. By all accounts Corax created a course to help ordinary members of the public defend themselves in court disputes, as their lands were being stolen during the reign of the tyrant Thrasybulus. Legend has it that Tisias was somewhat of an ingrate and tried to use the skills Corax taught him to avoid paying for his studies.

Tisias argued that Corax should sue him if he wanted payment, and if Tisias was unable to defend himself, Corax had taught him nothing and should not be paid. And obviously, if Tisias were to win, Corax would still get nothing.

Corax argued that he had taught Tisias everything he knew about the rhetorical arts and it could not be Corax's fault if Tisias were too unintelligent to make proper use of that knowledge. Therefore, Corax should be paid. If, however, the court were to find in Tisias's favour, that should be sufficient evidence that Tisias had learned his lessons well, and thus Corax should also receive proper payment.

The judge could find no fault with the logic of either party and was forced to dismiss the case.

Source: Nightfly

Corax was followed by other Greek luminaries, such as Protagoras, Gorgias and others, who were termed Sophists. They added more structure to the art of arguing a case, and from this we get the word sophisticated. If we fast forward through another half century, we encounter renowned philosophers such as Isocrates, Plato and Socrates, who was associated with forensic questioning; the bane of many a college student. Let's give the philosopher and teacher Aristotle a closer look.

ARISTOTLE – THE GRANDFATHER OF PUBLIC SPEAKING

Aristotle is important because he is credited with being the inventor of classical training in public speaking. He is regarded as the 'granddaddy' of public speaking for three reasons:

1. He wrote extensively on the subject.

2. He was as smart as a whip.

3. He captured the essence of what it takes to be an effective speaker better than almost anybody else of his era – or since.

Many tomes have been written about Aristotle's life and views on winning audiences over, storytelling, drama and more, so I won't delve into all his writings here. Rather, let's take a look at what he had to say about the art of rhetoric and his thoughts on how marrying intelligence and character leads to greater persuasiveness.

Aristotle defined rhetoric as the available means of persuasion. He argued that there are three central elements that impact upon a speaker's persuasiveness, providing a rhetorical situation exists in the first place. That is, assuming there's a problem to be addressed, an audience that is both capable of doing whatever you want them to do, and with reason why they might do so.

The three elements are:

....

1. Logos – logical appeal

....

2. Pathos – emotional appeal

....

3. Ethos – the character of a speaker

....

Let's examine each in more detail.

'Logos' - logical appeal

A speech must make sense and appear logical to an audience if it is to hold sway. Clearly, we can't give Aristotle much credit for originality on this score, as few people would see this suggestion as anything less than a prerequisite for a winning argument. After all, every audience will form a view on whether a speaker's rationale seems sound and believable while considering whatever he or she has to say.

That said, arguments aren't always cut and dried, and not every claim you make will be indisputable, where everyone can see immediately whether you're right or wrong. When dealing with more complex or disputable arguments, like court cases, logical support may often be provided through a mixture of facts, assumptions, inference, and more.

In the most complicated of cases, such as arguments over the best ways to make national health services more efficient while producing better results for patients and maximising value for money, it's entirely likely that even the most solid of arguments might be no better than judged more right or less wrong than others. Nevertheless, let's take it as read that you're asking for trouble if you attempt to persuade others with arguments you can't back up with logic that your audience can accept or buy into.

'Pathos' – emotional appeal

While logical argument is certainly important, it's not enough to win the day. You must also connect with your audience at an emotional level to capture their hearts and minds. If your audience doesn't feel something after you stop talking, the chances they'll do anything are two well-known chances – little and none.

Salesmen will tell you that all purchases are based on emotional decisions. Whether you're deciding to buy an ice cream or a new car – a low or high involvement call – you have to make an emotional decision to part with your money regardless of what you are buying. Even though you'll likely spend a great deal more time determining whether you want to buy a car and what car you may ultimately acquire than a choc ice; make no mistake about it, you have to feel a need before you part with your cash.

But how do you achieve emotional appeal? It is most commonly created through helping your audience visualise what you're talking about and why they should care. For instance, envisioning what it would be like to hold or eat an ice cream (sometimes after a visual cue of seeing others chomping on one or signage) can be enough to prompt a purchase decision.

While facts, figures and information matter here, the use of analogies, metaphors, stories or other words that evoke sensory reactions are far more important. And when it comes to gaining interest in more complex ideas, look no further than the approaches Steve Jobs used when launching new products. He consistently focused on 'showing' his audience what they could now do and feelings this might evoke rather than wallowing in detail. We will return to how you can create emotional appeal many times during this book.

'Ethos' – the character of a speaker

OK, so you may cobble together logical arguments and suitable forms of emotional appeal, yet you still might fail to persuade others if your audiences don't trust you. How many politicians do you know that fall into this category? Estate agents? Bankers? What about other walks of life? People who have made promises and not kept them? How about people you believe have attempted (even in small part) to pull the wool over your eyes? If you believe others have let you down like this once before (or many times), how likely are you to trust them later? You're not, right? It's difficult to win people over if you lack credibility.

Audiences don't just make judgements about whether an argument makes sense and how they feel about what you say, they also make assessments about whether you are someone that tells the truth or can be relied upon, and we use many different ways to make this call.

Your perceived credibility as a speaker can be affected by your audience's reactions to what they already know or have been told about you, as well as what you actually do and say. So if you're billed as a Professor of XYZ, or an expert who's been working in a given profession and industry for years; your audience may assume you know a great deal about your topic. However, you still need to prove it once you start talking.

Of course, if you haven't been doing something for ages, showing an audience that you (a) know where they are coming from, (b) have done your homework and (c) have something relevant to say to them will help to boost your credibility. The flipside of this is that an audience may ignore or even turn on you if they get so much as an inkling that you might be less than honest, or are trying to manipulate them.

Interestingly, Aristotle argued that logic was the most important of the appeals a speaker should possess. That said, a speaker who can combine all three appeals is likely to be far more persuasive, and many argue that credibility is more important than ever for any would-be leader in today's world.

So let's fast-forward about 2,500 years and to some practical applications for today's world.

> While logical appeal is vital, you must also connect with an audience at an emotional level to capture hearts and minds.

CHAPTER THREE

3

SPEECH BUILDING BLOCKS: AUDIENCE ANALYSIS

"By failing to prepare, you are preparing to fail."

Benjamin Franklin

So, you know that a speaker needs to have logical, emotional and credibility appeals in their arguments to be persuasive, but where do you start your journey towards swaying an audience to your point of view? There are three essential building blocks you'll need to consider and address before getting into the whole process of developing your arguments. These are ARC:

- Audience analysis
- Relevance
- Credibility

Each of these is vitally important and will have a significant bearing on the degree to which any audience is likely to be receptive to your ideas. This chapter and the next two will examine these in detail.

WHO IS YOUR AUDIENCE?

The Roman orator Cicero aptly advises 'before beginning, plan carefully'. Your first job as a speaker is to do your homework regarding who you'll be speaking to, as this should direct how you create your speech. In reality, most audiences will be made up of many different types of people, and while they may have some things in common, you'll rarely have just one category of audience to appeal to.

> **To exceed audience expectations, address problems you 'know' they care about.**

So how do you cope with the fact that you could have quite a few different audience categories sitting in front of you when you get up to speak? Here's a checklist of what you need to know:

1. Who are these people?

2. What are they expecting?

3. What do they know or believe?

4. Are your points actionable?

5. What might they expect of you?

Consider, for example, President Abraham Lincoln's second inaugural address in 1865.

Paying attention to needs of entire audience

Picture the scene. Abraham Lincoln is getting ready for his second inaugural speech. America is a nation torn apart by a civil war that has dragged on for four long years. The death toll on both sides of the fighting has been horrendous. The South is facing ruin and the North isn't in much better shape. There are huge problems with drought and food shortages, and there is great concern about what the future may hold.

With defeat of the Confederacy virtually assured and many on the pro-Union side actively seeking the apportionment of blame, retaliation and even vengeance, Lincoln could easily have joined in with these views and adopted a triumphalist tone or words... echoing the thoughts of so many of his supporters.

But instead, he chose to pay attention to the needs of his entire audience – those for him and those against. He knew that finger pointing would be a fruitless task, and it would only undermine his ability to convincingly lay the groundwork upon which reconciliation and healing could begin. He crafted words that spoke to the pain endured by all, forgiveness and a common belief in the providence of God's will as a basis from which a new beginning could be forged:

'With malice toward none; with charity for all; with firmness in the right, as God gives us to see the right, let us strive on to finish the work we are in; to bind up the nation's wounds; to care for him who shall have borne the battle, and for his widow, and his orphan - to do all which may achieve and cherish a just, and a lasting peace, among ourselves, and with all nations.'

WHO ARE THESE PEOPLE?

It is important to recognise that you'll rarely have just one type of audience you need to influence when addressing internal groups. And you're likely to face an even broader selection of audiences, with different needs and agendas, at external events such as conferences and seminars.

This begs an obvious question; given that you'll plan to make just one speech, how do you speak convincingly to a group composed of multiple audiences?

Start by identifying the common reasons that bring all these people together? For example, it could be:

- An AGM or EGM where certain decisions need to be made.

- A board or management meeting where corporate results, strategies or ideas may be up for discussion, review and/or decisions.

- An industry forum, seminar or conference put together to address specific topics of interest to certain industries or disciplines. These can vary from events that examine issues in great detail or at a more general level, and it's usually going to be somewhere in between.

Regardless of why people turn up to listen to speeches or presentations, it would be folly to assume that your speech should only address one element within an audience. But more on this later.

WHAT ARE THEY EXPECTING?

Even if the reasons for people getting together are self-explanatory, i.e. the title of the event is clear-cut in meaning and/or the agenda is tightly defined, you may find different audience members turning up with different expectations. But how will you know what these range of expectations might be? If you know the people, you'll find it much easier to make assumptions about what different people may be interested in. On other occasions, you may need to do some research.

If you don't know who'll be in your audience (and this happens more commonly than you may think), a good starting point would be to ask whoever is organising the event about invitees and confirmed attendees. They'll commonly know quite a few things – names, companies, roles, where they're from geographically – and given that they organised the gig, they should know what topics people are getting together to discuss.

Then there's the certainty that your audience won't want you repeating some (or worse still, all) of what other speakers have to say. How often have you had to sit through a seminar or event and listened to the same ideas repeated over and over again? Tedious, isn't it? This is entirely avoidable through a little bit of research. So do yourself and your audience a favour, and check out what any other speakers are likely to talk about – and make sure you have something different in mind, ideally offering more value to your audience than the others.

In addition to finding out what else will be discussed, check out a few more things rather than making assumptions about your audiences' expectations:

- What is the title of the event?
- What problems should it help solve?
- What decisions could your audience take as a consequence of attending the event?

It is worth noting that many audiences will have very limited expectations from an event based on their experiences in the past. Let's face it, far too many speeches underwhelm audiences, even if well thought out and delivered, because they are not actionable.

Far from being depressing, this is actually great news, because it means you can appear a bit of a hero if you exceed some fairly limited expectations. After all, how good do you feel when have been somewhere expecting little or no reward and you have a positive experience?

This is an important starting point for all speakers. Set out your stall to exceed audience expectations first time and every time.

WHAT DO THEY KNOW OR BELIEVE?

How sophisticated or knowledgeable do you believe your audience will be? Will they know more, less or about the same amount on the planned topics as you do? Given what you believe they know, how should this influence what you say? For instance, if your audience knows very little about the subjects you want to present, what groundwork will you need to lay before making your arguments? On the other hand, an audience won't thank you and may actually switch off very quickly if you pitch ideas at a level that is too basic for them.

The truth is different people are convinced or persuaded by different things. The factors that make a difference include:

- What people know, either from personal experience or because they believe such things to be facts.

- What people believe, based on observations and/or perceptions.

While most of us tend to place more store by personal experiences, trusting our own judgment, we also place surprisingly great store by information we have read, seen or heard from third-party sources we trust. For instance, you've probably never been to the North Pole and yet you almost certainly have a view of what it might be like there. We rely on reported facts and external information (often from the media) to interpret much of what's happening around us and globally.

As a speaker, it's in your vested interest to understand as much as you can about what your target audiences believe and why (including the sources they trust), as these will shape the attitudes and behaviours you want to influence.

ARE YOUR POINTS ACTIONABLE?

There's little point in addressing any group of people and encouraging them to do something they are unable to put into practice. If you are arguing that certain decisions should be taken and the people you're speaking to don't have the authority or capacity to make such decisions, it's just a waste of time. Furthermore, even if your audience includes the right people to address a given problem, maybe there is no budget or manpower to do anything about the issues you highlight. Or perhaps other obstacles, constraints or competing priorities mean that it won't matter whether people agree with you or not, because nothing can or will happen.

Clearly, if you decide to press on heroically in these situations (regardless of whether your audience agrees with you or are on your side), you're only going to spin everyone's wheels – and what's the point in that? Not only is this not good for you, it may also result in you wasting credibility capital you could well do with for other occasions! Indeed you can avoid any pain in this regard by establishing whether an exigency exists. If one doesn't, action is unlikely to be possible, even if the audience were suffused with enthusiasm to do so. Don't panic, that's simply a posh academic term for saying: Is there a problem that:

- Is capable of being tackled?
- Some/many people in your audience could do something about?
- Has constraints that can actually be overcome?

See chapter 12 for more about these points.

WHAT MIGHT THE AUDIENCE EXPECT OF YOU?

In the same way that you make assumptions about what your audience may expect from the event and/or elements within it, you also need to consider what they may be expecting of you. Do audience members know you, or what have they been told about you? What level of expertise are they likely to expect or associate with you? Where do you fit into the grand scheme of things within the event? Are you expected to act as:

- A featured speaker?

- An expert?

- A moderator?

- Someone who will instigate discussions?

- A problem solver?

- One or more of these hats?

Knowing what people expect of you will make your life much easier as you plot a course to meet or exceed their expectations. It's good to know these things, because it's always much easier to play to and leverage an audience's expectations of you than to try to build a new persona in their eyes.

CHAPTER FOUR

SPEECH BUILDING BLOCKS: RELEVANCE

"The single biggest problem in communication is the illusion that it is taking place."

G.B. Shaw

Having done your homework regarding your audience, what they know and what they might expect, your next job is critical. You have to approach whatever you say to your audience from their frames of reference and not yours.

One of the most important lessons public speakers must grasp from the get-go is that a speech or presentation is never about you, the person who is addressing those assembled. There may be an 'i' in speaking, but it is absolutely not about you. The only people who need to find your messages relevant are those in your audience. You don't need to convince yourself.

There may be an 'I' in speaking, but it's never about you.

There are four things you can do to achieve greater relevance:

1. Determining your audience's starting points.

2. Identify why your audience should care about your ideas.

3. Appreciate where communication comes from.

4. Leverage interaction.

BUILD FROM YOUR AUDIENCE'S STARTING POINTS

Centre your speeches on problems or choices that matter to your audience and what you want them to do. Do this before setting out the journeys you want them to take. To determine the core message you want to share with your audience, answer this question: What do you want your audience to understand, feel and do after you sit down?

Then, consider what journey your audience may need to take to reach these conclusions from their current attitudes, perceptions and capabilities. Think about the following:

- What do they already know about your idea?
- What do they think about it?
- How can you couch your message to build upon audience assumptions or perceptions?

The last thing you want to do is to pitch ideas at a level where your audience won't get what you say because they cannot. The flipside is also true; you don't want them dismissing your arguments because the points you make are too basic or lacking in weight. This is where your audience analysis comes in handy. If you are pitching ideas that are technical in nature to a non-technical audience, or making assumptions that an audience possesses certain knowledge they do not, you're on a one-way ticket to disconnection with your audience.

IDENTIFY WHY YOUR AUDIENCE SHOULD CARE ABOUT YOUR IDEAS

Here's a certainty about every audience you will ever address: they will care more about things that matter to them than about you. My sales director in one of my previous business ventures used to take great delight in explaining to me: 'People never buy for your reasons, they buy for their own' – and the same thing applies to public speaking.

This is not to say that people in your audience will always be self-absorbed (far from it), but understand that it will be difficult to become a great speaker if you fail to focus on

'WIIFM' on behalf of your audience. This stands for 'What's In It For Me?' and it's so important to both understand these words and take them to heart. We all gravitate most towards ideas and people who act in our vested interest and engage in things we care about. If your audience can't see how they will benefit from adopting your ideas, you're going to have an uphill battle to inspire them to take any action.

In determining these benefits, take the time at this stage to both:

- Describe what arriving at your recommended destination might look like for your audience.
- Define, as specifically as you can, what they might gain from that experience.

APPRECIATE WHERE COMMUNICATION COMES FROM

As a speaker, your job is to ground everything you say and do from your audiences' perspectives. Here's something you should know and think about, but it may seem a bit illogical at first. Just as people will be more motivated by things that benefit them (from their frames of reference), communication never comes from you to your audience – it can only come from your audience! Here's why.

It doesn't matter how much sense the language you use and the messages you want to share with others make to you. If you speak of things that don't matter or don't make sense to your audience, little or no communication can occur. To take an example that exaggerates the point, if you address an audience using an ancient Italian dialect and they don't speak the same language, it's obvious that your messages can't possibly get through.

This is one of the most important lessons for all public speakers. Your job is to persuade your audience and not yourself. Pay attention to how you can make your language and ideas more accessible to your audience. Always start from where they are and not from where anyone else might want to believe they should be. Consider, for example, Prime Minister Tony Blair's response to the death of Princess Diana in 1997.

Persuading your audience

It happened in the early hours of 31 August 1997. Princess Diana was in the back seat of a car that went out of control and crashed in a tunnel in Paris. Five hours later she was pronounced dead. Now, imagine for a moment that you were an adviser to the British Royal Family at the time.

What would you have advised Queen Elizabeth to say in the aftermath of this dreadful tragedy? Would you have supported a traditional tack of decorum, stoicism, duty and protocol, especially given that Diana was no longer officially part of the Royal fold?

Tony Blair took a different approach. Later that day – reacting to the sense of shock, numbness and outpouring of grief throughout the length and breadth of Britain, including an endless stream of people assembling and leaving flowers, cards, pictures and more outside the gates of Kensington Palace – he emotionally sought to capture the mood of the public and addressed the cameras by saying:

'I feel like everyone else in this country today – utterly devastated. Our thoughts and prayers are with Princess Diana's family – in particular her two sons, the two boys – our hearts go out to them. We are today a nation, in Britain, in a state of shock, in mourning, in grief that is so deeply painful for us.... She was the people's princess and that's how she will stay, how she will remain in our hearts and in our memories forever.'

LEVERAGE INTERACTION

Research shows that people remember and learn about things in different ways. So, where appropriate, finding ways to help your audience to feel more involved in presentations can greatly increase both how much they recall and how much they'll do about it afterwards.

You can be certain of some things, almost regardless of audience:

- Words will be forgotten almost as soon as they are spoken.
- Pictures are easier to understand and recall later than words.
- Interaction is better still when you want people to recall anything.

Why is this? Well, just think back to when you were in school. Which were you more likely to remember, the things you heard or the things you did? The latter, of course, as applied learning is almost always going to have greater impact than information you receive passively. To quote a well-known Chinese proverb: 'Tell me, I'll forget. Show me, I'll remember. But involve me and I'll understand.'

Part 3 will discuss these aspects in greater detail.

'Tell me, I'll forget, Show me, I'll remember' and 'Involve me, I'll understand'.

CHAPTER FIVE

SPEECH BUILDING BLOCKS: CREDIBILITY

"To be persuasive we must be believable; to be believable we must be credible; to be credible we must be truthful."

Edward R. Murrow

Credibility matters, for without it trust will not follow. Whether you are addressing a large or small audience and there are minor or major issues at stake, audiences have to reach a point where they see you as someone who should be believed and believable. Audiences are unlikely to be receptive to speakers who lack it. Look, for example, at how Barack Obama came to be seen as a serious contender for President of the United States.

Becoming a contender

He was hardly a complete unknown. After all, he had won a State Senate seat twice in Illinois since 1997 and gained some kudos for his unsuccessful bid to become a Congressman in 2000 on behalf of the Democratic Party. His name was Barack Obama and he was chosen to give the keynote address at the Democratic National Convention in July 2004, supporting the nomination of Senator John Kerry for the Democratic Presidential ticket.

Despite his relative inexperience and the fact that he was not a household name, this speech is widely acknowledged as the launching pad from which his successful bid to become the first black President of the United States just four years later was born. This was the day that Obama's credibility was truly confirmed on a national stage.

But where does a speaker's credibility come from? There are many sources, but these three are in my opinion the most important:

....

1. Your title

....

2. Your known experience

....

3. The impression you create

....

Your title

If you're introduced as a professor of nuclear physics, there's a good chance your audience will expect you to know a thing or two about nuclear physics. This is a halo effect, where people may assume that you have a particular expertise because of a title. Mind you, there can be grades of authority associated with a title. For instance, the level of credibility accorded to you may depend on the degree of expertise associated with your specific title – just think about the titles, consultant, specialist, general practitioner, registrar, and junior doctor. Whose hands would you prefer to place your life in? For those who value academic credentials, a title from one university may be seen as more prestigious than another from a less well-known or lauded establishment.

Leaving aside the source or inferred rank of a title, audiences will commonly assume you to be a trustworthy source of information or knowledge if your title suggests you have expertise on a given topic. Of course, you could have earned your title a long time ago, or you may not have devoted much time to the exact topic at hand, so truth be told, you will still need to show that you know your stuff. However, an audience may be prepared to give you a longer period of time in which to establish that you're worth listening to than someone else who does not possess your credentials.

Your known experience

A more common form of inferred authority is that gained by people in the course of their work or other activities, where their knowledge is accumulated over a lengthy period of time by doing things. So if you've been involved in developing a certain form of software for years, or you have become an old hand at doing something, this has a value too. And this is especially true when you are speaking to your peers. Your experience can open both doors and ears. Audiences tend to appreciate those who have been there, done it, got the t-shirt and are still wearing it!

The halo effect of known experience can even outshine that of a title. In many circles, knowledge accumulated by doing things is perceived to offer greater value, because solutions proposed by these speakers may offer the prospect of more practical and less theoretical application. Obviously, the opposite can occur if an audience feels they are about to spend time with an old stick-in-the-mud, who has been doing things a certain way forever and is not up-to-date with the latest ideas and developments.

So, just because you have experience in a given area, it doesn't mean an audience will gravitate towards your ideas. However, a bit like having a title, due to your experience an audience may indulge you a little longer than might otherwise be the case until they decide if they like or care about what you have to say.

So long as you do have the right experience, there are various ways to establish this halo effect. These include providing biographies and pre-event marketing materials, pre-event content, introductions, and during a speech itself. By doing so, you are favouring a show versus tell approach. Later in the book, in chapter 7, I will return to the do's and don'ts of when and how you can benefit from this form of trust from an audience that may not know about your experience. This in turn will boost your credibility without appearing to be self-serving.

Conversely, a perception of inexperience can sometimes turn into a bit of an advantage. This is because it's almost always easier to exceed limited expectations than to meet or approach high ones! Think of it this way; have you ever gone to a film, a play or a concert where you didn't know much about what you would see or hear? You may have found yourself approaching that event with a very limited expectation, where any experience that breached boredom would actually be a result! And how often in this situation have you found that you have been pleasantly surprised? Maybe the premise of the movie might have been a bit artsy, and yet you found that the ideas you saw struck a chord with you.

The very same can apply to presentations when delivered by a relative novice. It depends on you. With your ideas, you can provide much value to audiences and turn the ship around, changing their minds and earning their undivided attention. A lot will depend on the impression you make.

The impression you create

The impression you create is actually the most important form of credibility. Even if you have a title or 25 years of experience in XYZ to boast of, audiences will still assess or reassess whether they believe or trust you within moments of first seeing and hearing you. You have to demonstrate that you understand where your audience is coming from and what they need. So what exactly are audiences looking for? Basically, knowledge, something they value, and sincerity.

KNOWLEDGE

This is all about showing how you know what you're talking about. Do you know what you're talking about? Is it evident? How do you show your audience that you not only understand a topic, but can also relay your knowledge to them in meaningful ways?

As a speaker you need to demonstrate that you've done your homework and can translate your experience and knowledge in practical and meaningful ways for your audience, especially through the use of examples. The latter is important, as a greater focus on show versus tell will almost always provide a more inspiring and memorable experience for your audience.

SOMETHING THEY VALUE

Audiences may vary in many ways but they have one thing in common – they turn up to listen because they expect to get something out of the experience. Therefore, most audiences will more than warm to you if you can meet or exceed their expectations.

If an audience feels better off after a presentation than they were before, they will be delighted with that speaker, and his or her credibility will be enhanced. So centre every talk on issues you know matter to your audience and how you can provide value to help them deal with these matters. If an audience senses you're on their side, playing for them and obviously selfless, you're onto a winning performance!

Regardless of good intentions, as a speaker, never show up without having figured out why what you have to say is worth hearing by those sitting in front of you. No one appreciates having his or her time wasted, and not only will speakers who commit this offence fail to command attention the first time they do this, but they also run the danger of being ignored later at future events. After all, once bitten, twice shy!

SINCERITY

Here's a note of caution. You can be quite an expert on a subject, say all the right things and still not be rated as credible. If your demeanour or style smacks of arrogance or self-aggrandizement, of not caring about your audience or just being generally self-absorbed, this will make your audience bristle. People rarely react well to a 'know it all' or someone full of their own self-importance, and audiences can react against people they do not like. This is where Aristotle's ethos comes to the fore.

Perceived character counts just as much as real character. Be in no doubt that audience members tend to have an instinctive 'sincerity detector' that they use to make conscious and unconscious decisions about speakers. These are the same instincts humans have used throughout the ages to assess potential threats when meeting others, and making those all-important and difficult friend or foe determinations.

If people don't buy into you, don't find you trustworthy or are concerned about your honesty, they will be far less likely to take action on the back of whatever you say. So even if people subscribe to your logic and even feel quite passionate about the emotions you have stirred, inspiration will commonly not be turned into application if they don't like or trust the guy or gal encouraging them to do something. It's human nature.

How often have you seen politicians fail to garner support for an idea, even if they are 95 per cent or more correct in their assessment of a situation and can suggest plausible solutions. This happens all the time, doesn't it? So make it easy for others to feel they can trust you, by obviously caring more about the welfare of others than of yourself.

You're now ready to get creative. In the next few chapters, I'm going to bring you through a step-by-step approach to write more compelling speeches, building on the foundation we've worked on in Part 2. Let's begin.

> Manage your reputation as a speaker. It's valuable. Deliver on promises made about you and your talk every time you speak.

PART 2: HOMEWORK

INFORMATION TO GATHER ABOUT YOUR AUDIENCE BEFORE WRITING A SPEECH

When asked to speak at an event, be fully briefed about who's going to be there, what the event is about, and audience expectations. Get in touch with the event organisers, and maybe even select event attendees to help you assess how to exceed what is expected of you.

1. The event:

a. What's the event called, if it has a name?

b. If the event has a central theme, what is it?

c. What is the main purpose of the event?

d. When and where will the event be held?

e. What's on the agenda on the day you're to speak?

f. What related events will precede and/or follow it?

g. What formats will be used during the event and for what purpose?

h. What outcomes do the event organisers hope to achieve through the event?

2. The audience:

a. Who will be there?

    i. Who are they (ages, gender split, level of seniority, from what industries and/or occupation types, etc.)?

    ii. What range of knowledge and expertise is the audience likely to have regarding the topics you will address?

    iii. What are the top 2 to 3 challenges they commonly need to tackle regarding your topic?

    iv. What other challenges or issues will members of your audience be most focused upon?

  b. What are their most important expectations from the event?

  c. What are they likely to know about you and expect from you?

3. Other speakers:

  a. Who else will be speaking on the day?

  b. What will they be speaking about?

  c. In what sequence and in what formats?

4. Your speech:

  a. How much time will you have to speak?

  b. Are there specific issues you are expected to address?

  c. What, if any, topics do you need to avoid or treat with sensitivity or tact?

  d. What other speakers have spoken to your audience regarding your topic in recent years?

    i. If any, what was the nature of information they shared?

    ii. How will what you have to say be different and of value?

  e. Have you spoken to some, many or all of this audience before regarding this topic?

    i. If yes, what will you say that will be different and offer the audience equal or greater value this time around?

CHAPTER SIX

HOW TO CONSTRUCT A COMPELLING SPEECH

"Argument is meant to reveal the truth, not to create it."

Benjamin Franklin

Now we're moving to the point where we begin to construct a compelling speech. You have done your preliminary homework on who your audiences are, what they do, what they care about, and their expectations. And you've given thought to how what you want to promote might be relevant to them, from their perspectives, and what it may take to boost the trust they'll place in your message and in you as a speaker. But you're not going to write your speech quite yet.

IT'S ALL IN THE PREPARATION

Like a top chef preparing to deliver an irresistible dish, you'll need a few things before you start cooking. You'll need a mouth-watering recipe and the finest ingredients before you make a thing. In speech-preparation equivalents, you'll need to assemble engaging content to add to a winning structure and a big idea.

However, unlike a chef, your job as a speaker is to lead and inspire others to act rather than to do everything yourself. Your purpose must be more about creating a speech to address 'what's, whys and so what's' than to drill into lashings of detail. You are there to facilitate audiences reaching their own conclusions rather than spoon-feeding or dictating.

But, before I address the steps you need to take to prep yourself for writing speeches, it's important for you to understand a few things about public speaking. Speeches and presentations are ideally suited to:

- Creating an emotional connection with your target audiences
- Exciting them about ideas, as they see possibilities (from their viewpoints)
- Inspiring action
- Engendering trust

However, they also have a number of important limitations you need to work around and leverage. All of these are related and require you to favour emotional triggers and connections over detail. They include:

1. **Time**. In most cases, the amount of time you'll speak in front of an audience is short. You mustn't waste your audiences' time or yours. See chapter 15 for more on time management.

2. **Attention spans**. Getting audiences to pay attention for large tranches of time has always been tricky. And it's actually getting worse.

   In an era of unprecedented information overload, attention spans have dwindled to a matter of seconds rather than moments. And the upshot is that most of us find ourselves filtering or ignoring information we don't find immediately interesting.

   Further, even where you do a great job in commanding audience attention, research shows you're likely to face stifled yawns and glazed expressions if you speak for longer than 10 minutes without using audience involvement techniques. We'll discuss this quite a bit later.

In the meantime, the moral of the story is this: if you lose or never gain audience interest, you'll have a heck of a job getting it back later. So make sure you keep your talk focused. Steer away from content that competes with, dilutes or derails clarity and engagement.

3. Memory. An audience's capacity to remember what a speaker says is far smaller than most people realise and needs to be managed for better results. Simply put, if people don't remember what you said, nothing is going to happen after you sit down. What a waste of everyone's time.

> Think simplicity when you speak. Simplify before you amplify.

MEMORY – THE HARD FACTS

Let's get more specific. Research shows that the following happens after a typical speech:

- As soon as a speaker sits down, audiences will struggle to remember more than 50 per cent of what was said.

- Within 24 hours, people won't recall more than 25 per cent of what you said.

- A week after your speech, if you were really interesting and engaging, your audience is unlikely to recall more than 10 per cent of what you said.

However, startling as these figures may seem, there's good news. You can achieve a better result if you make it easier for your audience to recall your ideas. And the best way to do this, whether you speak for 5 minutes or an hour or more, is to limit every speech to just one central theme, which for your audience is worth remembering and visual in nature.

Do not hit your audiences with many messages. They can't and won't remember them. In fact, every extra message you include in a presentation will decrease your audience's ability to retain (and ultimately act upon) previous messages in a disproportionate fashion. Additionally, your theme must strike an emotional chord with your audience.

Why is this so important? While scientists have still much to learn about human memory, a number of things are clear. You need to work with the three stages adults go through to remember anything:

1. ENCODING

This requires you to earn your audience's attention, albeit fleeting, for long enough to attach meaning to what you say. And for the most part, this happens through the creation of visual images in our brains. 'Vision is memory,' according to Aude Oliva, research scientist at the Computer Science and Artificial Intelligence Laboratory at Massachusetts Institute of Technology (MIT). If the brain can't see what you mean, no meaning occurs.

2. STORAGE OF SHORT-TERM MEMORIES

Getting people to attach meaning to what you say isn't enough. They also have to make an instant decision, conscious or unconscious, that they care about it enough to bump something else and put it into their short-term memory.

As John Medina, author of Brain Rules, explains: 'The brain remembers the emotional components of an experience better than any other aspect... Studies show that emotional arousal focuses attention on the "gist" of an experience at the expense of the peripheral details. Many researchers think that's how memory works – by recording the gist of what we encounter, not by retaining a literal record of the experience.'

And if your audience feels they'll have to work too hard to attach meaning to or create associations with what they've just encountered, you're on a one-way ticket to being forgettable. Conversely, the simpler and more emotion you evoke with your message, the more likely you are to get past this stage.

3. RETRIEVING MEMORIES

If memories aren't retrieved and put to use, they're useless – right? You want your audience to feel that they can put whatever ideas you shared with them to good use quickly either by themselves or through others. The fresher the memory, the easier to follow up and the bigger the payoff. And the more likely it is that your audience will do something with it. The upshot – and this applies to each of these limitations – is that you must 'ditch details when you speak' and think like the makers of great advertisements.

Simplify, Simplify, Simplify. Amplify, Amplify, Amplify.

Think more like a writer of short stories than novels when you speak. You don't have time to get off-point, to lose steam or have your audience wonder what you mean.

CONSTRUCTING YOUR ARGUMENT

The three elements to speech development are:

1. Define a cornerstone to focus your audience on what you'd like them to understand, believe and do.

2. Use structure to give your arguments shape, clarity and direction.

3. Add content to make your words engaging, inspiring and memorable.

Central focus of your speech

While each of the above elements is fundamental and should be addressed in order, none is more important than the focus of your talk. Aristotle and his cohorts referred to this arena as 'topos' and renowned Roman orators like Cicero and Quintilian called it 'locus'. It's basically about finding the seat of your argument or the place from which it can be found. And as you'll have gathered, it matters. If you aren't clear about the central argument you want to make, there's a racing certainty your audience won't be either.

So your first job as a speaker, first time and every time, is to clarify what you want your audience to understand, believe and to act upon. You simply don't have a more important job to do. Without this step, your speech is destined to be rudderless and ineffective. Accomplished speakers regularly spend more time on this task than almost any other part of their speech development processes. Rightly so. This is a make or break time. Get this wrong and you'll struggle to persuade. Get it right and you'll find it easier to centre your speech and set it up for success.

As communication expert Dianna Booher likes to say: 'If you can't say what your speech is about in a minute, you sure as heck won't say it in an hour!' If there is any possibility that your audience will struggle to understand anything you say or have to work too hard to 'get' what you had in mind, start over and simplify.

SIMPLIFY BEFORE YOU AMPLIFY

Now that you know your audience won't remember more than 10 per cent of what you say, wouldn't it be a good idea if you decided beforehand what that 10 per cent should be? Bear in mind that you want your audience to get three things during your presentation:

> ## Audiences won't remember more than 10% of what you say a week after you speak. Decide what that 10% will be.

1. What was it about?

2. What's the main point to be taken from your ideas?

3. What can be done with that information?

This requires you to condense your central points into just a few sentences. Here's an example. I want to convince you to limit yourself to just one central point in every presentation from now on.

What's my main claim?

> 'People won't remember more than 10 per cent of what you say whenever you speak!'

And the main benefit of knowing that?

> 'If I focus on and keep building upon the 10 per cent I want people to remember, my audience is more likely to recall my essential idea.'

And the action?

> 'Limit every future speech to just one main point.'

The implicit payoff for my audience is that they'll be better off than if they receive a multi-message-strewn speech, where they mightn't have remembered anything at all!

If marshalled correctly, people will remember the essence of what you say later so long as you make it easy for them to do so. It must be active, never passive. And remember the advice of Winston Churchill: 'If you have an important point to make, don't try to be subtle or clever. Use a pile driver. Hit the point once. Then come back and hit it again. Then hit it a third time – a tremendous whack.'

SPECIFIC QUESTIONS TO ASK AND ANSWER:

- What do you want your audiences to understand, feel and do after you finish speaking?
- Where is your audience starting from regarding your topic?
  - o How knowledgeable or experienced are they?
  - o What is their disposition towards your topic?
  - o How much of a priority is this or could it be?
- What journey do you believe needs to be taken to reach your goal?
- If they adopt your ideas, what will the result or outcome look like to them?
- Why should they care?
- What might stop or hamper them in taking this journey?
- What resources, including skills, will they need to implement your ideas and how readily attainable are these?

After determining your answers to the above, you now need to boil it all down to one central theme based on where you want your audience to be after you finish speaking and what that might look like. If they remember nothing else, what is it you want them to bring away for themselves and to share with others?

Limit yourself to one phrase and as few words as you can manage. Think headline, think benefits to your audience (WIIFM), think action and think simplicity.

> ## What do you want your audience to understand, believe and do? Create a one-page speech overview to create a clear, concise and compelling argument

Here's an example. This is a variation of a real theme shared at the AGM of a well-known public company in 2013.

What the CFO (who shall remain anonymous) said:

'Achieving a reduced reliance on short-term funding instruments is essential to facilitate a more sustainable liquidity coverage ratio, more acceptable costs of funding and greater confidence amongst our trade creditors regarding the financial viability of the business.'

What he meant:

We need longer term funding so:

- We can continue to trade with current suppliers.
- We can afford our funding costs.
- We can make some money.

And the actual message the audience needed to take away was:

....

'We can grow with long-term money or die without it.'

....

When it comes to examples of first-rate message control, there are few speakers who outshone Winston Churchill during World War II. His 'We Shall Fight on the Beaches' speech in June 1940 is a particularly fine example of how limiting an oration to one central theme, direct words and emotional appeal created a winning formula. The simplicity of his message – that Britain will fight to the death against Nazi tyranny – made it easy for those who heard his words to get his point, to take them to heart, to remember them and share them (with little loss of meaning) to others who didn't hear his speech.

And did his words have an effect! They were literally a tonic for the troops and public morale in the immediate aftermath of the Dunkirk evacuation and the fact that Britain was virtually defenceless – not least because of the vast amount of materials and armaments left behind in France while fleeing the German army. In essence, he created a battle cry that galvanised a nation with much needed hope to carry on while all around them things were falling apart.

The focus on simplicity was also strategic to Steve Jobs, former CEO and co-founder of Apple. A favourite mantra of his at Apple appeared in an advertisement for one of the earlier Mac computers: 'Simplicity is the ultimate sophistication', a quote attributed to Leonardo da Vinci. His relentless focus on simplification was great news for those who bought Apple products; they consistently delivered better experiences with less hassle for their customers than their competitors' products. As a speaker, you would do well to take a leaf out of Steve's playbook. Simpler messages and words are easier to get and adopt. So do resist complexity at every turn; it will merely breed resistance, apathy and/or inaction.

WHAT HAPPENS IF YOU HAVE MORE THAN ONE MESSAGE YOU'D LIKE TO SHARE?

This is a common concern for speakers who believe they should make full use of the time available by cramming it full of useful information to more completely cover whatever is to be discussed on the day. For many of us, when asked to speak about something, we feel the urge to share what we know, and if we're experts on something, that could to be a lot. Resist this temptation. Remember, audiences cannot and do not multitask. In speaking, less is more.

Building a powerful structure

Having settled on a central theme, you now have a solid platform around which you can develop your speech. Your next step will be to create a structure or outline you can use to distil and shape your thinking, helping you to create a clear, concise and compelling argument before you start to add content.

Like a painter who sketches out ideas before creating a masterpiece, you should use structure as a tool to assemble and marshal thoughts. It will help you to organise what you want to say to your audience – to invent and test the quality, strength, and likely impact of the elements you want in include your speech. Once you're satisfied that your overall outline argument is solid, from start to finish, you're much more likely to create a coherent speech that will inspire confidence.

WHAT DO YOU NEED?

In the canons of rhetoric devised by Cicero, this part of speech development was called arrangement, known as disposito in Latin or taxis in Greek. Rather than give you textbook or academic definitions of the steps Cicero and Quintilian would recommend you take – including the exordium, narrative, partition, confirmation, refutation and peroration, all still valid today – here's an easier list of questions to answer:

1. What is your central message or argument?

2. Why is what you say true? What proofs or evidence can you offer?

3. What examples can you give to illustrate why each of these proofs are valid, helping your audience to 'see' what you mean?

4. What are the main concerns or issues some or many of your audience members may have about your message? Why do they feel this way? And how would you address their concerns?

5. What conclusions do you want your audience to reach?

6. What actions do you wish them to take as a consequence?

As you consider each of the above, and recognising that you have already reached a conclusion regarding the first of these questions above, this is a good time to mention the value of a back of an envelope! Many speaking professionals, myself included, will use a small piece of paper to sketch out the answers to these questions with the express purpose of limiting what is said in each response to as few words as possible. The smaller the space you allow yourself, the more succinct you have to be.

Download a **FREE** template you can use for this purpose at **www.howtomakepowerfulspeeches.com**

THIS IS A LITMUS TEST FOR YOUR SPEECH.

- Does your outline argument appear solid, clear and compelling to you?

- Are there any elements of what you've written – amounting to a mini-version of your speech – that you need to strengthen or replace to make a stronger argument?

- If your audience believes and accepts each of these elements, would these be enough to persuade your audience to draw and act upon the conclusions you'd like them to reach?

o Adopting or supporting your ideas because they believe this would be worth their while?

o Clear about the actions they should take next?

o Capable of sharing these ideas with others not present, who you also hope to persuade?

Keep editing your outline until you reach a point where you feel it's as tight and clear, on point and meaningful to your audience as you can make it. Understand that this will form the core of what your audience should glean from your speech and remember later. Consider the following sample speech outlines.

SAMPLE SPEECH STRUCTURE 1:

President John F. Kennedy Inaugural Address, 1961

Central message:	We must start anew our quest for freedom and human rights for all – at home and elsewhere.

Proofs and examples:

1.	The ideal of liberty in America and elsewhere is under threat and it's now our job to enable, maintain and fulfil that promise.
	Illustration: 'We're ready to make it happen' pledges/commitments to those who support our interests and those who don't – contrasting benefits of working with other nations for common good versus the downsides of failing to do so.

2.	America and the Soviet Bloc must work together to avert the threat of war, terror and oppression.
	Illustration: Contrast benefits of possible paths towards conciliation, common interests and peace versus dangers of oppression, poverty and a war that could destroy mankind.
3.	The path won't be easy but 'we' must take steps or make sacrifices to lead the way to what is right.
	Illustration: Contrast why you (we) must be selfless and dedicated to God's work as if it was your own versus favouring a self-focus. Together we can achieve a greater good.
Counter argument:	Why are you appeasing those who wish ill to America?
Rationale:	You are showing weakness.
Rebuttal:	You can't make an omelette without breaking eggs. The price of the distrust and impasse between America and the Soviets is too high to pay. A new start must be made to foster belief that negotiations between the two superpowers can yield fruits versus entrenchment of division.

SAMPLE SPEECH STRUCTURE 2:

A Fundraising Appeal to Help Combat Effects of Intellectual Disabilities

Central message:	Transform lives. Support efforts to tackle severe intellectual disabilities in children.

Proofs and examples:

1.	The more severe the case, the more difficult it is for families to provide needed care by themselves. *Illustration*: Story of Donal, an eight-year-old boy with an intellectual disability. Include fears that he would not communicate or understand his family and the stresses, worries and consequences parents (and other children) experience in giving a child like this the one-on-one attention he needs.
2.	Therapies, if made available, can offer vital hope to families. *Illustration*: Story of remarkable journey Donal made with specialist support in just six months, including an ability to engage more with others and to take part in and enjoy social experiences.
3.	Forums for families to share knowledge between each other and give encouragement are a godsend. *Illustration*: Many families caring for

	a child with intellectual disabilities feel alone and isolated. Personal examples of how support forums make a difference include helping families to learn from others, to persevere, and to strive towards achieving more.
Counter argument:	Why not accept your children's limitations?
Rationale:	You run the risk of causing more upset and stress by striving after things you don't know can work. Why do it?
Rebuttal:	Every child has the right to love, happiness and fulfilment, and to reach their full potential, whatever that might be. If we don't try, we'll never succeed. Together we can lighten the load, do more and create new possibilities.

COULDN'T USING A STRUCTURE MAKE A SPEECH OVERLY FORMAL?

This is a concern for many people who worry that using a structure might stifle their creativity, mess with their flow or even constrain their thinking. You may be of a 'Christopher Columbus didn't need no stinking map, and neither do I!' mindset.

However, structure actually helps a speaker to be more creative and to apply creativity where it's likely to count. It creates a platform from which a speaker is likely to express himself/herself in a more pleasing and memorable way. As leadership guru Steve Denning said in a 2011 Forbes article, 'creativity must have structure'.

Create content to keep audiences engaged

The third element of speech development is creating content to make your words engaging, inspiring and memorable. This is dealt with more fully in the next chapter.

Creativity and structure

I believe structure is necessary because structure and creativity have the same parentage. It is structure that enables creativity. We see examples of this everywhere. In nature, we see the fantastic diversity generated by a few basic structural elements: no more than a hundred varieties of atoms and a couple of primary colors lead to a universe of infinite beauty and diversity. In the great human creations, in the twelve notes of the musical scale, in the twenty-six letters of the alphabet, these fantastic structural inventions have unlocked the enormous creativity of literature and music. Without structure, there is nothing for creativity to get leverage upon.

Source: Steve Denning, 'Creativity Must Have Structure', Forbes, 29 March 2011

CHAPTER SEVEN

DEVELOPING CONTENT

"People don't buy for logical reasons. They buy for emotional reasons."

Zig Ziglar

Having focused your speech on a single, compelling idea and supported it with a powerful argument structure, it's time to amplify these for effect. This is the part where – before you write your first full-draft speech – you need to:

- Flesh out the content you plan to include in your speech and determine what material you should leave out.
- Make some important decisions about emphasis, balance and evidence required to bolster your arguments.
- Sketch out your overall plan of attack.

While your outline contains the essential components you'll want to deliver through your speech, now you need to develop your storyline, paying attention to:

- Content squad decisions
- Integration of persuasive appeals – your mixture of logical, emotional and character based appeals
- Your story flow from the beginning to the middle to the end of your talk

CONTENT SQUAD DECISIONS

Like a manager of a top football team who makes calls about team selection and the best approach to each game, including who should be in attack, defence or on the reserves bench and tactics to be employed, you need to assess and prioritise the material you have at your disposal. This is necessary in order to make your ideas more accessible, persuasive and engaging.

An easy way to do this is to grab a few blank pages and jot down – in a broad-brush or topline fashion – answers to the following questions for each of the proofs, examples/ illustrations and counterarguments you plan to use:

- What's your essential point or conclusion for each?

- What range of facts, assumptions or inferences do you have at your disposal to back up the accuracy of what you plan to say?

- If your audience accepts the point you make, what are the conclusions this should help them to reach?

Review your answers to the above and determine:

- What you must, could or don't need to refer to during your speech.

- Are there areas or gaps where you need to locate or assemble more or better information to make a more engaging argument? If so, where can you source this and/ or what do you need to do to bolster your material?

- Do you have material that you won't include in your talk but may need to heed when preparing for question and answer sessions? (I'll discuss these further in chapter 10.)

Your purpose at this point is to sift through content you can use to bolster and bring your speech to life. You need to jettison anything that really doesn't add to your central arguments. Padding or tangents should be noted and dropped at this stage. You're aiming for a no-fluff zone, where you'll focus all of your attention on how you can help people to see and care about only the most vital of issues, concerns or ideas. And in the process you won't be dumping any data on your audience or expecting them to make any hard yards to figure out what the important stuff was in your speech.

INTEGRATION OF PERSUASIVE APPEALS

The next step is to build or support your arguments. You need to provide proof of your claims, and second, you need to give people examples or images that can help them better understand and remember the points you make. One of the most important rules of public discourse is to help people see what you say is true. The foundations of truth you use to back up your arguments must be obvious.

For this we must revisit Aristotle and his three elements of persuasion: logos, ethos and pathos. Although you absolutely need to focus on emotional appeals to get and keep audience attention, cause them to care about your ideas and action them, this doesn't mean that you should focus on emotional connections to the extent that you neglect or ignore logical and character based appeals. Far from it. You need all three elements working together, with the balance dictated by your assessment of the journey you believe your audience needs to take.

CHARACTER TESTS, ETHOS REVISITED

Let's start with character and a quote ascribed to Aristotle by Eugene Garver, author of Aristotle's Rhetoric: An Art of Character: 'Do not speak from calculation, as they do nowadays, but from moral principle.'

The point Garver extracted from this and other similar cautions by Aristotle is this: audiences will not only assess your character by what you say, but also based on their assumptions about why you said it. As he so neatly put it: 'character is what makes us ascribe moral qualities to the agents.' As a speaker, your ability to sway audiences depends hugely on whether your audience trusts you. If not, as mentioned earlier, some or all of what you say will be disregarded.

So as you assess your potential content at this point, you should make it your business to ensure that it is free of art or even hints of manipulation. You want to be satisfied that what you say is likely to be seen as honest, open and, better still, selfless in nature. It will help make your arguments more convincing. Furthermore, it is more likely to make you appear to be a credible source of information.

Simply put, the more an audience feels they can place trust in you and your motivations, the more open they will be to buying your messages.

LOGIC AND THE RULE OF THREE

When it comes to figuring out how much proof you should provide to back up your arguments, I recommend that you start with the Rule of Three. It has been around forever, long before Aristotle and those who followed him, and its application can be found in almost every form of communication. And all because it works.

In storytelling, we talk of a beginning, middle and end. In plays you typically have an Act I, Act II and Act III. In children's tales, you'll find it in everything from 'The Three Pigs' to 'The Three Bears', in novels like The Three Musketeers, and so on. In joke writing, the rule of three, or the comic triple, is one of the most common formulas you'll find, consisting of two statements following a certain pattern, followed by something unexpected.

And in speech making, it has been a stock in trade for celebrated speakers throughout the ages and still to this day. For instance:

- Veni, vidi, vici (I came, I saw, I conquered) – Julius Caesar

- Friends, Romans, Countrymen – Mark Antony

- Blood, sweat and tears – Winston Churchill

- Yes we can, yes we can, yes we can – Barack Obama

It is widely held that if you say something three times, people will believe it to be true. If one statement of proof is a start, two are more convincing; three can seal the deal, being deemed more complete. After that, extra proof commonly doesn't add much more weight to whether people believe you or not. And remember, people can only absorb so much information.

There is another virtue to seeking at least three proofs for what you claim. Not only will you find that your arguments are convincing for others, but you'll likely boost your own confidence as well. Persuade yourself. If you know you're right, you're likely to be more convincing to others. Incidentally, this rule applies not just to your primary evidence for whatever you argue, it can also be brought to bear when backing up or explaining the constituent elements of your argument.

BACK TO PATHOS AND TAPPING INTO EMOTION

The most important element of examples you give to back up or demonstrate your arguments is that it must help your audience to 'see' what you mean. Remember Aristotle's pathos? And while I'll get to the role that humour, stories and visual aids can play in this regard within the next few chapters, together with some lessons you should learn from screenwriters in the way your speech unfolds, here are a few principles I recommend you adopt to boost your emotional connections: Think Meaning. Think Journey.

Of all the senses that people are likely to remember, visual imagery is top of the pile. You may remember from earlier that all purchase decisions are emotional ones, whether buying a car or an ice cream. We have to feel a need and be willing to invest something (time, money or energy) in satisfying that need. For bigger items, like a car, we may take quite a few things into account, such as price, colour, appearance, brand name, size, mileage, safety features, etc.

We may not make an immediate decision. But the decision to buy a car requires an emotional trigger, something that sets us off in the first place.

In order for you to do something versus nothing regarding your existing behaviour, or to replace what you use today for any reason, you will almost always need an emotional trigger to set you off. So we need to figure out what emotional triggers would be relevant to your target audiences. These could be anything from helping them to see that whatever they do or use today isn't a patch on whatever you have in mind, or something else.

The examples you use should collectively help your audiences to visualise what you have in mind, how it relates to them, and what it means (from their frames of reference, not yours). You need to make it easy for them to see how they can get the emotional benefits you describe, by including something they can do now or soon (as in immediately after your session), which can set them on the road to the promised whatever.

And whether you use stories, analogies, metaphor, your job is always the same. It's to help your audience to create visual signposts and experiences they can use to see or imagine how things might be for them if they adopt your ideas, what they might have to do to access this, and why they should care.

The greater the meaning and perceived emotional payoff you elicit, and the more your audience can see how these ideas apply to them, the more likely it is you'll spark emotional triggers that will incite action.

And the upshot? In fleshing out each example you plan to use, ask yourself how it can be couched to boost your audience's ability to find 'personal' meaning and applications. Let's look at how the next point can help you achieve this effect.

EMBRACE THE POWER OF SPECIFIC EXAMPLES

The more specific your examples, the more engaging your ideas will be and the easier it will be for your audience to tell your stories to others – as both will find more parallels in your words that are meaningful to them, their lives and their aspirations. But understand that creating topline visual ideas will rarely achieve the effect you want. After all, if you 'tell' your audience, for example, that 'Ireland is a beautiful country to visit' versus 'showing' them specific examples, guess which will be more memorable? Showing beats telling every time.

Taking another example, professional fundraisers for charities will tell you that their target audiences typically want to know three things before they'll give any money:

- What are you intending to do?

- Why does it matter?

- How much do you want from me and what'll this achieve?

Describing these things in broad-brush terms is a mistake. More specific examples are far more meaningful. For instance, which of these ideas would you be more inclined to support?

a) Let's reduce the scourge of prostate cancer, affecting 1 in 6 men over their lifetime.

b) John was just 42 when he passed away from prostate cancer. He didn't know about it until it was too late and now his wife Mary and their three children, all under the age of six, have lost a loving husband and father. Their world will never be the same again. Worse still is the knowledge that 4 in 5 men survive prostate cancer when it's diagnosed at an early stage. We need your help to screen, etc., etc.

Incidentally, using more specific examples like this isn't about manipulating an audience. Rather, you're making it easier for your audience to put themselves into the scene you create and imagine what they'd do, how they'd feel and what this might mean to them. You're making it easier for them to inject meaning into your words.

> Make the examples you use as visual as possible. Think connection and meaning

COMPLETING YOUR STORY FLOW

As you get ready to craft a speech, it helps to think of your entire talk in the context of an overall story. This includes where your story begins, what happens and how it concludes, i.e. your beginning, middle and end. And while there any many ways in which engaging stories can unfold, better stories tend to have certain elements in common:

• They begin with an introduction to a situation.

• Characters are faced with problem or challenges.

• They act and/or react.

• There are consequences.

• This is followed by more action, reaction, and upshots.

• A resolution or outcome to the journey unfolds.

As you know, you're not writing a novel or tome; instead, you need to adopt the mindset of a short story writer when you pen your talk. Given the limited timeframe available to you, you need to get attention from the get-go, never let go and focus hearts and minds on conclusions and specific actions they need to take later. That's it. Avoid detours.

And pivotal to this task is to bookend the content elements you've now determined you want to share with a great start and a rousing end. Let's look at the first of these jobs: hooking your audience and gaining their attention.

GET OFF TO A QUICK, COMPELLING START

In his review of thousands of movie scripts which worked and which did not, legendary screenwriting guru Syd Field claimed that if a story didn't grab his attention within the first 10 pages, it never would. He was of course right. However, as a speaker, you don't have the luxury of anywhere near that much time. In practice, you need to grab attention from your audience within the first 30 seconds of speaking.

What does it take to hook an audience that quickly? Simple. The prospect or promise of something that's worth their while. Your opening salvos should whet your audiences' appetites, encouraging them to sit up in eager anticipation of what may follow. The last thing you want to do is to blow this precious, make or break time with generalities, platitudes, thanking a gazillion people or talking about you and how wonderful you are. You need to start as you mean to go on with a focus on your audience and what's in for them. Begin with the good stuff, something they'll care about.

Of the many methods you can use to get attention from your audience, here are four techniques I suggest you consider putting on the top of your list. Each of these – followed by an example of its use in famous inspiration speeches – can individually or in combination with each other be used to cause your audience to want to know 'what happens next?'.

A. A STORY

While I'll get into a broader examination of when and why you should use stories in the next chapter, the secret to using a story at the outset of a speech is to start it when something is happening and make sure the point of the story reinforces the essential reason why your audience needs to listen to you.

For instance, Winston Churchill used story to quickly engage his audience about events that had unfolded which would require Britons to take resolute, immediate and even desperate measures in the face of Nazi aggression in June 1940.

> From the moment that the French defences at Sedan and on the Meuse were broken at the end of the second week of May, only a rapid retreat to Amiens and the south could have saved the British and French armies who had entered Belgium at the appeal of the Belgian king, but this strategic fact was not immediately realised.

B. A PERSONAL ANECDOTE

The following is a variation of the first example and can help an audience to see the speaker in a vulnerable and open light, engendering trust while still telling a story and making a point. It is taken from Nelson Mandela's speech from the dock, 'An Ideal for which I am Prepared to Die', in 1964. However, make sure you never use this in ways that could seem self-serving.

> I am the first accused. I hold a bachelor's degree in arts and practised as an attorney in Johannesburg for a number of years in partnership with Oliver Tambo. I am a convicted prisoner serving five years for leaving the country without a permit and for inciting people to go on strike at the end of May 1961.

C. A BOLD STATEMENT, CLAIM OR FACT

This can be a great way to stop an audience in their tracks

at the outset of a talk to think about something, providing of course it's true. For instance, supposing you began a talk about how to avoid illnesses caused by obesity. Your opening words might be:

> Adding just 30 minutes of moderate exercise into your daily routines can dramatically increase how long you'll live.

Is an opener like that likely to get attention from most people in an audience? Would it cause them to sit up and want to know more? Probably. And here's another example of this powerful tack used in the most famous of speeches from the last century. In Dr. Martin Luther King's 'I Have a Dream' speech, it suggests the audience are about to make history that day in 1963:

> I am happy to join with you today in what will go down in history as the greatest demonstration for freedom in the history of our nation.

A variation of this approach is to use a statement to shock or jolt the audience, commonly as a preface to persuading them that a big decision or change is required. For example in President Franklin D. Roosevelt's 'Pearl Harbor Address to the Nation':

> Mr. Vice President, Mr. Speaker, Members of the Senate and of the House of Representatives: Yesterday, December 7th, 1941 - a date which will live in infamy - the United States of America was suddenly and deliberately attacked by naval and air forces of the Empire of Japan.

D. START WITH A QUESTION OR TWO

Finally, this is favourite way to start a speech by many top speakers. This is because asking a question tends to cause audiences to consciously and unconsciously consider how they could answer your question. However, key to it are questions that must be thought-provoking, where the likely answers must offer potential value to your audience.

So, going back to the question 'why you should exercise to improve your health' argument above, you could start this talk with a series of questions such as:

> How could adding just 15 minutes of exercise a day to your daily routines transform your life and health?

It's the same point, just reframed. Again, let's look at this technique in action in a few more ways. For example with the Boston abolitionist, William Lloyd Garrison, speaking on the death of John Brown in 1859, hanged for using force to free slaves in the South:

> God forbid that we should any longer continue the accomplices of thieves and robbers, of men-stealers and women-whippers! We must join together in the name of freedom. As for the Union – where is it and what is it?

A first cousin of this method is an inferred question, employed in this case by Barack Obama in his victory speech after the 2008 Presidential election:

> If there is anyone out there who still doubts that America is a place where all things are possible; who still wonders if the dream of our founders is alive in our time; who still questions the power of our democracy, tonight is your answer.

FINISH STRONG

If you want your audience to leave a room after you've spoken intent on taking your words to heart and acting on them, you have to close your speech with a bang, never with an anticlimax or banalities. You need to focus your audience on your central theme, why they should care and what you're asking them to do next. Consider how you might make this visual, memorable and easy to relay to others not in the room, emphasising, perhaps in different words, your core message through your talk.

Think promise (of how things could or should be) and think call to action. Leave your audience in no doubt about what needs to happen next. Make sure the latter is easy and worthwhile to your audience.

Here are several great examples from home run, inspiring speeches that illustrate how it should be done. The first one is taken from Abraham Lincoln's 'House Divided' speech in 1858, concerning the nation's crisis over slavery.

··

Did we brave all then to falter now? - now - when that same enemy is wavering, dissevered and belligerent? The result is not doubtful. We shall not fail - if we stand firm, we shall not fail. Wise councils may accelerate or mistakes delay it, but, sooner or later the victory is sure to come.

··

In 2013, former President Bill Clinton concluded his speech at the 'Let Freedom Ring' ceremony to mark the 50th anniversary of the March on Washington:

> So how are we going to repay the debt? Dr. King's dream of interdependence, his prescription of wholehearted cooperation across racial lines - they ring as true today as they did 50 years ago. Oh, yes, we face terrible political gridlock now. Read a little history; it's nothing new. Yes, there remain racial inequalities in employment, income, health, wealth, incarceration, and in the victims and perpetrators of violent crime. But we don't face beatings, lynchings and shootings for our political beliefs anymore. And I would respectfully suggest that Martin Luther King did not live and die to hear his heirs whine about political gridlock. It is time to stop complaining and put our shoulders against the stubborn gates holding the American people back.

In 2006, one of my favourite speakers, Sir Ken Robinson, author of Out of Our Minds: Learning to be Creative, closed his TED speech about why schools need to nurture creativity, not compete with it, with the following stirring words:

> What TED celebrates is the gift of the human imagination. We have to be careful now that we use this gift wisely, and that we avert some of the scenarios that we've talked about. And the only way we'll do it is by seeing our creative capacities for the richness they are, and seeing our children for the hope that they are. And our task is to educate their whole being, so they can face this future. By the way, we may not see this future, but they will. And our job is to help them make something of it.

And more memorable still are the final words taken from President John F. Kennedy's inaugural address in 1961:

....

> And so, my fellow Americans: ask not what your country can do for you - ask what you can do for your country. My fellow citizens of the world: ask not what America will do for you, but what together we can do for the freedom of man.

....

See chapters 8 and 9 for more about using stories, humour, PowerPoint and visual aids.

Command audience attention within 30 seconds of speaking. Use questions, stories, facts and statements. Close every speech with a BANG.

CONTENT DEVELOPMENT ADVICE YOU SHOULD IGNORE

Have you ever come across advice that suggests you should employ a 'tell them what you're going to tell them, tell them, and tell them what you told them' approach within your speeches? To many, it can seem that this framework offers plenty of focus and repetition to reinforce ideas being shared. And since the adage is used so often, it may even sound like it has a ring of truth to it.

But, the truth is, it's utter nonsense. This is a formula that'll bore the bejinkers out of most audiences from the outset. Once you've told an audience what you're going to tell them, you're likely to lull them into inattention. After all, they know what's coming, so why bother? And that's a monumental problem.

CHAPTER EIGHT

CREATING ENGAGEMENT, INSIGHTS AND MEMORIES

> "A joke is a very serious thing."

Winston Churchill

So you've made calls on content, fleshed out what you plan to say, and delved into detail that might make your examples more effective. You've also given thought to how you can both command attention from the outset and inspire action from your audience through a rousing end to your talk.

Next up is a more detailed look at how you can mould your examples to build on the attention you win at the outset of a speech. It entails regularly reigniting attention and building support or interest in your arguments and what they could mean to your audience.

This is the part where we talk about upping engagement with your audience, helping them to connect the dots between your examples and the messages you have in mind. Used well, your examples can act as lynchpins or pillars that will make it easy for your audiences to sit up and take notice and achieve 'aha' moments that result in:

- Insights
- Meaning
- Memories, and
- Action

But if you want to achieve all of that, you need to engage the right side of your brain: the parts that help people enlist their creative abilities to 'see' how they can link what you're saying to stuff that matters to them. And it helps hugely if your examples are entertaining.

Why? It's because we're more likely to latch onto and share ideas we enjoy hearing about than those that seem dull or involve hard work to absorb. So, entertaining? If that has you worried that you're expected to be a funny man or woman to keep people at the edges of their seats, worry not. As I'll explain shortly, that's not at the heart of how great speakers use humour to tell an overall story.

Before I get to a hit list of sources you can use to build up examples your audiences will likely enjoy, let's bust a myth about using humour in your talks.

THE ROLE OF HUMOUR IN SPEECHES

When you ask almost any audience to tell you about speeches they enjoyed, most will tell you that the speakers in question were, amongst other things, amusing. In fact, a very high percentage of our clients believe that being witty is an essential part of a speaker's role. However, this perception can be off-putting for many people who believe they will struggle to be funny or that it is not in their nature.

So, do you really have to be a bit of a comedian to be a good speaker? Do you need a terrific arsenal of jokes that you can blend into your presentation, plus the capacity to deliver these with aplomb? Absolutely not. The purpose of using humour in a speech is less about joke telling and more about making your messages more fun, more memorable, less intimidating and less threating.

As I'll discuss shortly, it's about educating while you entertain, not just entertaining your audience in general. And in the process it's about having your audience feel:

- You're less of a threat (in more trying situations).
- You're like them (which boosts their trust in you).
- They want to hear more (because it's a pleasant experience).
- This is worth sharing later.

And the beauty of using humorous or entertaining examples to make your points is they're all about showing over telling and audiences love them. A winning combo. Reaction to humour tends to be both physical and mental. When we laugh or smile, we feel physically well and release dopamine, which induces a natural high, enhancing our pleasure from an experience. No wonder we enjoy it so much.

Jokes and perceived threats

In the book *The Naked Jape*, one of Britain's best-known comedians **Jimmy Carr** and writer **Lucy Greeves** examined in great detail the hidden world of jokes – to find out what's funny and why. They explain that jokes are told to make others laugh and 'laughter is a release of tension on discovering that a perceived threat is not, in fact, a threat at all'.

They explained that 'joking' provides 'a coping mechanism that works because it acknowledges what a mess things are and celebrates that fact'. In other words, jokes help to tell us that things are all right, even when we or others slip up or fail in some way.

ENTERTAINMENT DO'S AND DON'TS

So what do you need to know? Let's get to some rules of play when it comes to humour, entertainment and engagement.

DO

- Educate and entertain.
- Tell stories.
- Use self-deprecation.
- Help your audiences to visualise what you want to say.

DON'T

- Attempt to be a joke-cracking comedian.
- Use humour of limited appeal.
- Be crude.
- Pick on audience members or make them the butt of your humour.

The latter two are very important. If anyone is offended or taken aback by what you've said, you're onto a loser. It can damage your credibility and isn't worth it. However, audiences tend to react well to people who tell stories against themselves. Let's look at some of these do's and don'ts in closer detail.

EDUCATE AND ENTERTAIN

When using humour, your goal is to educate while you entertain. There is no virtue in creating a situation where your audience is highly entertained but doesn't get any of the points you want them to get. Think of it this way – have you ever seen an advertisement that you thought was really funny, where you really enjoyed it but were surprised when you found out who made it? In other words, you didn't make a connection between the gag and the message or its source? Yes? What a waste of your time and the advertiser's money.

Humour is a fantastic way to capture interest from your audience while they are enjoying the experience. However, they must get the point if you want them to do or feel something later. Humour is not a verbal tickling stick; it is a route to enjoyment and memorability. Using humour should have a definite purpose.

Returning to the world of advertising, there are many great examples of advertising campaigns that integrate the way their ideas can help to solve a problem in a humorous way. These include Specsavers in the UK and E*TRADE in the US. In these cases, humour is used to illustrate what can happen when you don't solve a problem (poor eyesight), or how you can make seemingly difficult tasks (making investment decisions and trades) easy. But humour does more than entertain; it encourages an audience to be more receptive.

Associating humour with ideas makes them more likely to:

- Be picked up by your short-term memory (encoded and stored)
- Translated from short-term memory to long-term memory.

So, for those who say they can't be funny or are reluctant to try, bear in mind that finding ways to inject a little humour that has a point into a speech can be the difference between whether something is retained or not.

DON'T BE THE COMEDIAN

As a speaker, however, it not your job to try to be a funny person. This is just as well as there are very few people who are cut out to succeed as tellers of jokes. It's one of the hardest jobs in the world. Most comedians learn their craft over time, whether of the joke-telling variety or yarn-spinning guild – and sometimes a very long time. A typical apprenticeship for stand-up comedians takes many years and requires a gradual building up of material and stage time. And even they are under constant pressure to freshen up their material, running the risk that audiences won't find their new ideas funny.

If it seems like I'm steering you away from the world of comedy, you caught me. I am. The good news is that you don't have to worry about trying to compete with people who make getting laughs for a living. Nor do you need to compete with speakers who have developed routines over many years and who had far more opportunity to practise their funny ideas than you may have had. You do not need to be a comedian. That is not your job. What you do want to do is to use humour to increase the memorability and impact of what you want to relay to your audience. In other words, it's a means and not an end.

BEWARE OF USING HUMOUR OF LIMITED APPEAL

Unlike when audiences self-select to watch or listen to comedians with a style or brand of humour they enjoy, trying to get laughs out of an audience that is actually made up of many different audiences is a tough ask. Speakers may find that their audience is made up of young and old, men and women, people with a great deal of experience and those with precious little, city folks and those from rural backgrounds, etc. You simply can't assume that all these people will find the same things funny. So avoid using humour of limited appeal.

Don't create humour. Unearth it. Use humour to educate as you entertain.

TELLING JOKES

While stories have the capacity to be a much more effective communication tool than jokes, it doesn't mean that you cannot or should not ever use jokes. Of course you can. However, if you're planning on inserting a few jokes, here are some guidelines I suggest you bear in mind.

GOOD JOKES

- Keep them short.

- Make sure they have a point.

- Keep them clean.

- Starting with a joke is not the best idea.

  Steer away from telling jokes at the start of a speech. If you get a good reaction, you're only setting an expectation that there's more to come at this level, and that can be hard to maintain. Don't put yourself under pressure from the get-go. If you get a lukewarm or poor reaction, your audience may consciously or subconsciously feel deflated, perhaps assuming that they're in for a less than interesting experience. That's bad news, as it's hard to regain an audience's attention once you lose it or fail to gain it at the outset.

- Consider telling gags that have a point at the end of a speech.

  If a closing joke goes well, your audience will leave with a pleasant (and hopefully visual) way to remember the point you want them to absorb.

- Practise and select your jokes wisely.

  You know the old adage about jokes: 'It's all about timing.' Well, it's true, but it's also about giving audiences enough time to react to what's said or what they see.

TELLING STORIES

There is a much easier way to entertain an audience without anywhere near the same level of art, gumption or practice – and that's storytelling. Stories have been used since time began to hand down apocryphal tales from one generation to the next and to engage audiences. And the good news is we're all storytellers. It's almost impossible not to be, if you interact with others at all. Whether at home, at work or in social settings, every time we tell others what happened to us or to someone we know, we are telling a story. Often we even tell stories with a purpose, where we want those listening to us to be swayed towards a point of view, for example, maybe believing something was right or wrong, the best team won or lost or something else.

WHY TELL STORIES?

You can and should tell stories for six reasons:

1. They are a time-honoured way of sharing ideas and engaging audiences.

2. They are easy to remember and relate.

3. Stories are visual and evoke emotions.

4. They can combine entertainment with a point.

5. Audiences associate the value of the experience they gain from well-told, apocryphal stories with the storyteller.

6. Stories can yield some of the best laughs.

STORIES ARE EASIER THAN SCRIPTS

Have you ever felt a little stressed when trying to remember what you wanted to say to a group, but once you started to tell a story, you felt instantly more relaxed? It's not uncommon, and for good reason. We are used to telling stories, and we're much more focused on what happened than the precise words we use to tell them. Few of us need much prompting to tell stories about significant events that have happened in our lives – whether at work, home or in social circles. You'll also tend to find that it's more relaxing to share stories than facts, or what you may consider to be drier, less interesting information. And your audience, who will always enjoy stories, will tend to pay more rapt attention when they hear one begin. They are more likely to want to hear what the speaker has to say.

STORIES EVOKE EMOTIONS AND IMAGES

Stories have the capacity to capture imaginations and make us feel things. Let me give you an example. You could say that it's a story about a story.

Being boring

Many years ago, I attended an event that announced the creation of a new children's science museum in Ireland. The large gathering of adults, children and the press were to be addressed by Bertie Ahern, the then Taoiseach (Prime Minister) of Ireland.

Bertie turned up late and made his way to the podium looking a little flustered. He looked up at his audience briefly before diverting his eyes down to read a speech I assume had been written by one of his underlings. After less than 30 seconds, my eight-year-old son, standing only 10 feet away from the Taoiseach, turned to me and said in a very loud voice:

'Dad, he's really boring!'

Can you imagine it? The whole room, Taoiseach included, looked first at my son and then at me. Awkward! Three thoughts instantly came to mind:

1. Why me? This shouldn't happen to a parent...

2. You know what? He's right; he was really boring!

3. Atta boy, you tell him, because no one else in this room would!

As Bertie looked at me, he made a faint smile. But I'm not sure if it was a sympathetic look or a disdainful glance. I'll never know. He then went back to the job at hand and started to read again, and I like to think he did so in the knowledge that there was a good chance he was boring the heck out of his audience. But what else could he do? He clearly wasn't prepared to engage his audience in any other way.

Now, as you were reading my embarrassing tale, could you see in your mind – even in such a short tale – what was going on? Did you form pictures in your head of my son, of me, other audience members and the Taoiseach? Could you imagine yourself there? Did you imagine what the characters mentioned looked like and what they might have been feeling? Chances are you did. Stories, like movies, can transport us to another reality, absorbing our attention and evoking emotions.

STORIES WITH A POINT ARE FUN

This is vitally important. It's useless to share stories that entertain an audience but fail to have the desired effect. They should be centred on what you want an audience to understand, feel and/or do. If you look at the Bertie Ahern story, I used it to make the point that reading a speech will create a boring experience for your audience and cause them to disengage. It also might make the secondary point that unless you have kids in the audience, they probably won't tell you that you messed up, so you may not know what happened. Stories always need to make a point.

APOCRYPHAL STORIES ASSOCIATE WITH THE STORYTELLER

Learning to hone this craft can create halo effects for speakers that go beyond gravitating towards persuasive arguments. Now, if at this point you're thinking, 'I don't tell stories' or 'I'm not sure I'm much of a storyteller', don't worry. One of the great things about telling stories is that you don't have to be as precise as a teller of jokes. Getting the exact sequence, timing or punchlines right or telling them the same way each time isn't necessary. In fact, the last thing you want an audience to believe is that you're just engaged in a highly dramatic performance. This can come across as being contrived, and unless done really well, it can actually dent the credibility of a speaker.

STORIES CAN YIELD THE BEST LAUGHS

Stories that solicit the most laughs from audiences are commonly those about:

- Things that went wrong
- Embarrassing moments
- Stupid choices or decisions
- Unfortunate misunderstandings

But rather than trying to capture these things in jokes, which can be hard to tell and remember, stories are always more personal, have greater potential to carry a message or point and can greatly enhance the credibility associated with the speaker. They are much better suited to educating an audience while entertaining them than jokes can ever be. Stories which speak to failure or things that went wrong can greatly amuse audiences, but again make sure there's a point or moral to the tale.

SOURCES OF INSPIRATION

Finding ways to add humour to what we say can make quite a difference, but let's get back to what happens if you think you're not cut out to be funny. That's perfectly okay. Here are some of the most common comments or questions we hear from our clients:

- I'm only funny in certain circumstances.
- I'm not in the same league as comedians.
- Being funny comes natural to some people but not to me.
- I don't know how to tell stories.
- Where will I get ideas?
- What happens if I don't have any stories?
- But what stories am I going to use?

Clearly, many of these questions are related. They mostly arise because many people don't see, recognise or believe that they are already storytellers, or else they doubt that they have the capacity to tell stories as well as others might. Bear in mind that corporate speeches and presentations commonly run for 20 to 60 minutes. If you're planning on entertaining your audience through much of what you say, how much of a routine or how much material do you need? A lot!

PERSONAL EXPERIENCES

So where do we get ideas? From things we have done, seen, heard or experienced in some fashion. And of these, personal experiences are usually the simplest and best places to start. This is because it tends to be easier for us to remember and talk about things that happened to us. For example, what happened, how it came about, the result, how we felt, and what was the context. Plus, when we speak of things we did, we tend to be entirely believable as we can often actually relive the sequence of events in the story, almost as if we were going through what happened again for the first time. The only difference is that we are using a story to provide a window for our audience to watch it all occur with us.

THE MEDIA

Other sources might be things you've heard from others, in person or maybe via television or another media source; online sources are increasingly common. Of course, if your source for a story is the media or any third party, be careful if there's any possibility of bias by whoever produced the content. You may need to check your facts. What's happening in the media can also be integrated into your stories to make them more memorable. For example, if something is getting a lot of play in the news – maybe something to do with the economy, a political decision or gaffe, a sporting result, etc. – then you can link this to your story with an analogy.

These connections help an audience to achieve a better visualisation of what you want them to understand and believe, paving the way for more memorable and actionable points.

For instance, supposing you want to speak to your audience about the necessity for change, there's a good chance that you can find high profile news stories about those who are making changes or resisting them, and the consequences of whatever is happening.

Other sources of stories and humour can include television or radio panel shows or comedy sketches. The reason why you should consider tuning into these kinds of shows is that the participants are usually seasoned campaigners at working material into something that both gets a laugh and is visual.

Remember, almost everything that makes us laugh is either visual at the outset or requires us to create a visual interpretation. It's about creating a feeling. To that end, you can often really add to a story or point you want to make with props or pictures. As you may recall, people don't remember more than 10 per cent of what you say, but pictures can last for such a long time.

GIVE CREDIT WHERE IT'S DUE

If you do hear stories from others, including other speakers who can be a great source of material, be sure to acknowledge your source. The same applies if you use material from radio, television or online. To do otherwise is dishonest at best and stealing material at worst. If others saw or heard what happened and know that you're not the original source, failing to let people know where you got your story from isn't just bad form (which it is), but it's also damaging to your credibility. This is especially true if audience members believe you are trying to benefit from something that wasn't yours.

TECHNIQUES ON INJECTING HUMOUR

So we know humour is important and that it has the capacity to educate while you entertain, providing it has a point. We also know that by using stories, jokes or other tools you can help your audience visualise what you have in mind in ways that are truly memorable.

USE THE CASCADE OR RIPPLE EFFECT

The last thing you want to do is share your stories at a fast pace. The faster you speak, the less time your audience has to hear you. Comedians will commonly wait for a first audience member to laugh before they then glance at that person for a moment. Why? It's because they want to create a cascade effect.

The trick is to find ideas that can appeal to enough people in an audience that some (or preferably many) of them will start to laugh. Once this happens, those around them will likely smile and set off a cascade effect that can result in a room full of laughter.

You can create this cascade effect when looking at your audience as you speak, using occasional and often almost imperceptible nods to different audience members from time to time. This encourages both the people you look at to nod back to you (which means they're not asleep and more likely to be listening to you) and encourages those around your audience nodders to also nod (in reflective mode) and find themselves listening more as well. The time to do this gentle nodding bit is while you're pausing between sentences. Remember, good comedy is not all about timing, it's about pausing.

AUDIENCE INTERACTION – PHYSICAL ACTION AND FACIAL EXPRESSIONS

If you have happened to attend a comedy set in the recent past, stop for a second and see what you remember from that experience. Do you remember many specific stories or lines they shared, or would most of your memories have to do with how you observed the interaction between the comedian and audience? In other words, how you and the audience reacted to them and vice versa?

Even if you remembered quite a few gags (and, unsurprisingly, you're much more likely to have remembered stories than jokes), chances are that what you remember most was visual recall of what it was like to be there at the event, experiencing it again, in small parts, visually.

The use of facial expressions and even physical actions can greatly amplify the comedic effect of stories you tell. This doesn't mean that you need to run off and take acting lessons if you feel you're not naturally gifted in the animated face league. Nor does it mean that you should engage in any form of slapstick antics – far from it. Even limited efforts to physically 'show' your audience what is happening in your stories or your reactions to unfolding events can pay off handsomely. It can sometimes be the difference between whether people laugh or not, and here's why.

Visual information conveys meaning faster than your words. We're preconditioned to look at the faces of those we listen to, searching for visual cues to add context and meaning. No wonder almost all top comedians, past and present, use facial expressions to get better reactions to their material. From the blank stare of Tommy Cooper to the facial gymnastics of Rowan Atkinson, facial expressions convey meaning.

Those who look serious or concerned cause us to react differently than those we believe are joking. We will take in information from the reactions of those around us as well to check if our read is correct or should be adjusted. So if you're in a crowd who happens to be reflecting back to a speaker with smiles, well, what's a body to do?

By not rushing your stories and injecting short pauses between sentences, you will give your audience a chance to both keep up with your words and your body language. Just as audience members look at you while you speak, they also look at you while you're not speaking. They see your eyes, your gestures and your interplay with them – and of these, seeing your eyes is the most important.

Just think for a moment about how you interact with your friends. It's not just about chatter or banter, you also see the gleams or glints in their eyes and the natural ways in which their faces move to amplify stories they may tell you. You don't need to do any more than that as a speaker.

There should be nothing contrived about facial expressions, as it's unnecessary, not to mention hard to maintain. You just need to give people enough time to hear and see you. Then, let smiles and natural exuberance follow and see how cascade effects will do the rest. Above all, never try to force laughs.

Chapter 14 discusses pacing and pausing in more detail, while chapter 13 looks at body language.

CHAPTER NINE

USING POWERPOINT AND OTHER VISUAL AIDS

"A picture is worth a thousand words."

Napoleon Bonaparte

THE POWER OF VISUAL AIDS

Extensive research shows that depending on when and how you add pictures to the words you use, audience recall rockets upwards. As John Medina explains in his book Brain Rules: 'If information is presented orally, people only remember about 10 per cent, tested 72 hours after exposure. That figure goes up to 65 per cent if you add a picture.'

Obviously this won't come as a surprise to you, since you now know that visual cues are vital for memory. Or as Medina neatly puts it: 'We do not see with our eyes. We see with our brains.' Referring to the brain cortex, wherein we store long-term memories, he says 'there is no such thing as words'.

And the moral of this story? The only reasons you should use visual aids are: they must add to the impact of what you are saying, making it easier for your audiences to visually:

• Get your messages.

• Buy your arguments.

• Remember what you said.

• Imagine the consequences of acting upon your ideas.

That's it! De-emphasise words, and go big on being visual. But don't panic. This doesn't mean there is no place for words, but rather they need to be used sparingly and for maximum impact. Here's what you need to know about words used in visual aids.

MEANING ATTACHED TO VISUAL IMAGERY

When audiences see words in presentation slides, they have to read these and then visualise what they mean and attach meaning to them before deciding if they're worth encoding and being placed in their short-term memories. Worse still, realise that most of us take shortcuts when we do this. We choose to only recall 'bits' we feel are new and important. And, furthermore, we only pay attention, in the first place, if we can see a way to connect or associate new information with other things we know or believe.

Failing these, we can't be bothered. We will filter out things deemed low priority, as there is a limit to our short-term memory capacity in order for us to function and get anything done. In this process, we block out things we judge aren't needed. Cutting out the middleman, if you will. Naturally, you have to give consideration to what images you may want to use, what meaning you want people to take from these, and how you can make the point you want through pictures.

But pictures are often not enough on their own. They need to make a point, and you use words as signposts to shape the meanings you would like your audience to get.

But realise that any meaning associated with pictures, props, stories, gags, analogies, metaphors, etc. will not be decided by you. Each audience member will determine what, if any, meaning and importance they will attach to each of these things. That said, if you fail to help your audience to visualise your messages, then the chance of them remembering much is really small. And while they may recall the gist of your most important points, don't you owe it to your audience and yourself to make it easier for them?

Hailed by many as one of Barack Obama's greatest speeches, the following is a terrific example of a speech that is littered with visual imagery. These pictures were painted with words minus PowerPoint or visual aids.

This is your victory

If there is anyone out there who still doubts that America is a place where all things are possible; who still wonders if the dream of our founders is alive in our time; who still questions the power of our democracy, tonight is your answer.

It's the answer told by lines that stretched around schools and churches in numbers this nation has never seen; by people who waited three hours and four hours, many for the first time in their lives, because they believed that this time must be different; that their voices could be that difference...

I was never the likeliest candidate for this office. We didn't start with much money or many endorsements. Our campaign was not hatched in the halls of Washington – it began in the backyards of Des Moines and the living rooms of Concord and the front porches of Charleston.

It was built by working men and women who dug into what little savings they had to give five dollars and ten dollars and twenty dollars to this cause. It grew strength from the young people who rejected the myth of their generation's apathy; who left their homes and their families for jobs that offered little pay and less sleep; from the not-so-young people who braved the bitter cold and scorching heat to knock on doors of perfect strangers; from the millions of Americans who volunteered, and organized and proved that more than two centuries later a government of the people, by the people and for the people has not perished from the Earth. This is your victory.

Extracts from Barack Obama's victory speech for the 2008 Presidential election.

The election victory speech of Obama captures what it would look and feel like to have lines of people waiting to vote for three or more hours, many of whom had never done so before; the images of a campaign that was built from humble origins and the man on the street – the ordinary people who dug into their limited savings to fund his cause; the almost biblical pictures conjured by young people who left their families and survived hardship to join with him – becoming his apostles?; the way in which he hailed the heroic efforts of his foot soldiers who endured heat or cold to pave the way for more votes.

And why is this such a stand-out speech, causing many people, myself included, to remember where they were when they heard it and how it made them feel? It's because he used visual imagery that stirred emotions among his many target audiences, who could literally see and feel what he meant by his words.

THE LACK OF POWER IN POWERPOINT

When you hear the term visual aids, do you immediately think of PowerPoint?

According to statistics generally thrown about, there are an estimated 25 to 30 million PowerPoint presentations given every day. Incredible! But do you know what the unfortunate thing is? Despite the effort put into creating these presentations, almost all are destined to be nigh on useless! That's because the vast majority of PowerPoint templates encourage users to be text-centric and use too many words, and this is the last thing any presenter should want to do.

Templates suggest overly formulaic solutions. It's like an instant cookie kit you can find in the supermarkets – just add a little water, roll 'em out, turn on the oven and hey presto!

PowerPoint seems to offer a 'fill in the blanks' solution – just add words and the odd image or graphic here and there, and voilà! But stop right there. Think about what your audience needs rather than your convenience.

WE ARE CONDITIONED TO READ WORDS

If you share many words with your audience on a slide (and I'll come back to what constitutes 'many' in a moment), what happens once you crank up the light to project these pearls of wisdom onto a wall or other surface? Like a moth to a flame, your audience will turn away from you and start to read. You are now about to ask your audience to multitask – to read your words and listen to you at the same time. And here's the thing. Men and women can't multitask in this instance! If you're reading something, it's hard for you to listen at the same time, and even if you can or do, you will be less efficient at both. But it gets worse.

If you're asking your audience to read a host of bullet points, there are a number of things you should know. First, your audience can read whatever you threw up on a slide anywhere from two to five times faster than you will regale them about those words! Then, when they're done (having mostly not listened to you up to this point), they will commonly stop listening. Why? Well, if you've just read someone's slide, don't you think you'd believe you know what's coming from their explanation? Of course you would.

Most of us have a tendency to filter information and once we think we have the gist of something, we stop listening. Even if you limit yourself to three or four bullet points instead of the ten-plus-point brigade, you'll still have problems. Not only will your audience forget virtually every word you write, in most cases they have no clue as to which points they should retain (if they get excited enough) and they can't cope with them all. If you haven't highlighted the few words you want people to focus on, how can they attribute relative priority to one bullet point versus another? It's a toughie, isn't it?

WE DON'T RECALL WORDS

As you may remember, your audience won't remember more than 10 per cent of what you say. So how about the words we read? It's worse – grim, even. We struggle to recall more than 1 per cent of the words we read from slides.

SO, WHY BOTHER?

Okay, so you've got the point now. Presenting PowerPoint slides that are chock-full of words is a guaranteed way of ensuring people can't and won't remember what you have in mind. Why bother then? The reasons why people in their millions do this every day can vary from ease and habit to it's what everyone else does and it seems to be the professional way to share information. And while it may seem like it can help speakers to marshal their thoughts, don't use it for this purpose. Here's a better plan.

HOW TO DO POWERPOINT WELL

It is possible to do PowerPoint well by (a) only using it after you've created your speech (as a support act), and (b) applying a few simple rules.

THINK VISUALLY

Think in terms of stories rather than using slides as speaking notes. Instead of showering your audience with many words on slides, limit any words you use to create headlines that capture (in a few words) the essence of what you want your audiences to understand. Complement these with images which amplify the point you want to make.

Favour pictures over words on slides. They'll boost your emotional connection.

Let's take an example. Suppose you want to tell your audience that wordy slides are bad news. A standard PowerPoint presentation slide on this might look something like this:

Why you need to avoid wordy slides

- If you create slides with oodles of bullet points, your audience will read ahead of your speech and be distracted by trying to read and listen at the same time

- That's even before they grapple with any dodgy typography or colours!

- The outcome is likely to be 'word blur' or complete turn off

- Graphs and excel sheets that can't be read are guaranteed to lose the audience completely

- And a shockingly high percentage of slides are worse than this one!

The Reluctant Speakers Club. Aug 2013

A better and more accessible way to share these ideas with an audience might be as follows:

Why is this so much better than the all-word variety of the same ideas? Well, how long did it take for you to read the headline in the second example? Less than a second, right? And then what did you do? You looked at the supporting image, which reinforced or added further explanation to the words in the headline. Am I right? The total time you spent doing these things was negligible, and once you were done you would now be free to divert your attention back to the speaker.

Importantly, the words you read captured the important bits you're supposed to get. The speaker can now reinforce these core ideas and explain why they are of interest to you.

Adding the picture was important too, as this increased your ability to remember words by an extraordinary level. To reiterate, research shows that just 10 per cent of your words may be recalled. But when you add pictures, this rockets to 65 per cent within four days of when you spoke and 20 per cent in the longer term. It's a no-brainer. Add images that complement what you want your audience to remember but add words too, via headlines, as you weave your story.

THINK ONE POINT PER SLIDE

Make life easier for your audience. Don't be tempted to include busy graphical information to cover many different points. You may save on handout pages, but you will lose on comprehension and recall. De-clutter graphics that contain a lot of information, even if the graphic is on point.

If the point you want to make through images isn't immediately obvious after a glance, your audience will now have to study your slide more, while not listening to you. Or, on the other hand, they may choose to blank this part of your presentation altogether. Not a good plan.

CHOOSING FONTS AND COLOURS FOR EFFECT

Slides can be useful to amplify and reinforce your key messages, helping your audience to visualise your ideas and attaching a headline or verbal hook to your messages. But I also want to say a few words about fonts and colours. There are two rules I would suggest you adopt for words you present on slides:

1. Make them easy to read.
2. Use fonts and colours for greater effect.

Even with limited words, make sure your audience doesn't have to work too hard to read what you write.

- **Favour easy-to-read fonts**

   Verdana or Helvetica are ideal for overheads. These can be read more rapidly and are easier on tired eyes!

- **Don't use small font sizes.**

   Think headlines and think big.

- **Don't use light colours or dark backgrounds.**

   These can be distracting and mask your words.

- **Avoid clutter – more really is less.**

   Don't confront your audience with busy slides that are full of stuff. If your audience can't see at a glance, without explanation, what you want them to understand, you've failed. You won't save any time by using one slide to make many points.

USING PROPS

Providing you don't abuse props, they can be a wonderful means of helping an audience to both visualise your points and enjoy the experience of your explanations. Three is an absolute maximum in any presentation.

Suppose you want to make a point about the importance of reducing stress for the well-being of a workforce. You could use a pillow as a prop, and ask a few questions to help your audience to 'see' what you are getting at. You could ask:

- Do you rest easily at night?
- When you hit the pillow, can you switch off?

If you were in that audience and you were asked these questions, can you imagine how a simple pillow being used in this way might help you to visualise the points being made? Probably.

I remember the first time I saw someone using a prop to great effect, and I was highly amused by the experience. A woman from Texas made a dramatic entrance into an insurance industry conference in London wearing a blue magician's hat to a 'Pump Up the Volume' recording of Queen's 'It's a Kind of Magic'. The audience didn't know quite what to make of her, unaccustomed to hearing music at conferences. Most just sat there in stony silence, while others looked at each other, sharing glances of embarrassment on behalf of the speaker. Not a great start, you might think.

Despite getting virtually no reaction, the speaker didn't miss a beat. This is how she opened her speech:

....

> Well, I heard y'all were real reserved in jolly old England, so I thought I'd like to see if you could get excited about data management. You see I'm here to talk about a type of magic you have at your fingertips and may be ignoring.

....

Then she paused for a moment and, changing her tone, said:

> Everyone in this room has information you can use to literally transform your customers' experiences. You have a capacity to amaze them in ways your competitors probably can't or don't. Now, do I have your attention?

This was a very bold opening, but as she said these words slowly and with passion, you could see that she had indeed captured her audience's attention. The topic at hand was normally a dry one – data management and customer databases. But here was someone who had taken a different spin on matters. She had her audience at the edge of their seats as she talked about the possibilities of how customer experiences could be transformed into something special or magical, by merely paying attention to details that many companies had already captured about their customers.

That event was more than 25 years ago, and I still remember that speech and what she did through the simple use of a prop – a prop that many speakers wouldn't even dare to use, as it might make them look foolish. Used in moderation, props offer a terrific means of helping your audiences to really see what you have in mind. But again don't forget about the potential of pictures.

Going back to why props are so effective. I have a colleague, Yanky Fachler, who writes and speaks extensively on the subject of entrepreneurs and their mindsets. He likes to speak about the concerns many people have about risk, and how people can cope with uncertainty both for themselves and at a family level. And one of his favourite props is an old workman's ladder that he places in the corner of a room when he is presenting.

He typically leaves the ladder there and ignores it for at least 30 minutes. Then he'll point at the ladder and ask, 'Did anybody notice that old ladder there?' Of course he knows everyone did indeed notice it at some stage, and probably wondered who left it there. As people nod their heads, he climbs halfway up the ladder and begins speaking again.

> Where are you in your lives? If your life was like a building project, where do you think you would be in that project? Are you still heading upwards, or maybe you need to go back a step in order to climb one more step? Or maybe you're in two minds about what your next step should be?

The reason I'm sharing this vignette with you is that again, years after attending this presentation, his audience members remember the questions he asked and his imagery of life as a ladder, with decisions to be made about the steps we take. Even now, there's a good chance you've just created some mental pictures of the questions he asked and that old ladder. Powerful, isn't it?

Using props is not gimmicky unless you choose to make it so. It's a variation of the parables told of old, where we compare one thing to another to capture the essence of the point we want to make. Because the comparison is visual, we have cues that help us create new images that are meaningful to ourselves. And self-created images are always more memorable and readily acted upon.

Use props or low-tech visual aids to focus audience attention on key points. They greatly increase an audience's visual and emotional engagement with ideas.

USING VIDEO

In addition to pictures and props, one of the most obvious additional ways to create visual imagery for an audience is through the use of video, either your own or someone else's. Nowadays the cost and time required to create your own videos have fallen dramatically and, with the right script, practice and even basic kit, you can create some really interesting content.

This is great, but when and how can you use this capacity when speaking to an audience? Be careful, proceed with caution. Remember, when you speak with an audience you are there to engage with them, and to inspire and persuade them of your ideas. So any use of video should be to support instead of competing with these goals.

Here are three ways you can do just that with video:

- **Keep it short.**

  Using a video during a presentation requires an interruption, when you stop speaking and then have to re-engage your audience when the video is done. The longer your video, the longer you have been disconnected with your audience, and the more your video is doing the job you should be doing.

- **Favour stories over facts.**

  Although attuned to watching videos or visual media, the rules regarding what we're more likely to remember still apply. Stories are still more memorable that facts or 'more dry' information.

....

- **It's a support not a lead.**

  In most cases, you want the role of video to be that of supporting the main points you want to make. You typically don't want to rely on the video to make or 'own' the central arguments put forward, otherwise it begs the question of why or whether you need to be there. Are you just a support act? Clearly, if you created the video or play a lead role in it, there may be good reasons why you may want to give the video a more central role. But even if the latter is true, I repeat, visual aids of any form are there to support, amplify and complement the arguments you want to make, not compete with or even overshadow them.

NOTES

The question always emerges should you give your audience notes at all. The simple answer is yes. But as a rule of thumb, don't give out notes to your audience before you speak, even if event organisers ask you to do so. Here's why. Notes can serve an important function. Use them to help your audience remember the most important points you made and anything you want them to share with others. In other words, use notes as an aide-mémoire.

Make sure you tell your audience up-front that you'll provide notes after you speak, so they won't feel the urge to write notes as you go, which can also reduce attention to what you say. It's hard to write stuff down and not miss large chunks of what is said.

What's the first thing you do if given notes before a meeting? You scan or read them before and/or at the beginning of a speech. And guess what happens next? You will likely do one of the following:

- If the notes didn't interest you, there's a good chance you'll switch off before the speaker says a word. Oops.

- If the notes do seem interesting and you decide you do want to listen to the speaker, you'll still be hard pressed not to prejudge what you're going to hear. Since you already know the gist of what you're about to hear, you're not under the same obligation to pay attention to what follows.

The upshot of giving notes to your audience before you speak is that it encourages your audience to pay less or no attention to what you are going to say, and to you as the source of information. The latter is an especially bad idea. But if you want them to pay attention to you and see you as a credible source for the ideas you want to share or the actions you want people to take, then don't dilute their focus on you before you start. Remember, you are the source, and people need to find you engaging, credible and memorable for anything to happen after you speak.

CHAPTER TEN

HANDLING QUESTIONS AND COMMENTS

"A prudent question is one half of wisdom."

Francis Bacon

10

As a speaker it's not enough to just prepare your speech. You also need to ready yourself to answer questions that may arise from what you say. This isn't an extra piece of work, it's part of your total job at hand.

You don't want to do a great job of persuading your audience about your ideas, only to find your messages get compromised by a poor Q&A session. If you prepare well, you'll likely find questions arising from your talks will be less onerous and numerous. Nevertheless, consider and plan for how and when addressing audience questions can be integrated into your talk for best effect.

PREDICTING QUESTIONS

How can you put yourself in the best position possible and answer questions while keeping on message? Always think pre-emptively. Assuming you have put in the whole nine yards preparing a relevant and compelling speech, there's a good chance that you'll be able to make some fairly accurate assumptions about the range and nature of questions your audience might ask of you. More often than not, you can even predict the vast majority of questions that you might face.

Pay attention to the most important of these, and consider how you might both answer these questions and use them to bolster your arguments. If some of these questions could serve to materially undermine the points you want to make,

> Be ready to answer questions about what you say. This isn't an extra task; it's part of your overall preparation.

consider how to integrate these into your speech as you would other opposing points of view, acknowledging them and then countering them as part of your presentation. If you can do a good job in this regard, you will make your arguments stronger, and at the same time negate the capacity of others to dent or even destroy your ideas.

WHEN TO ALLOW QUESTIONS

Providing you've done your homework and you're comfortable doing so, it's a good idea to answer questions as you go or at designated times you select during your speech. This approach tends to be better than leaving questions until after a talk for a number of reasons:

- You're likely to be asked things that are more on point.
- Your audience will get more timely and engaging responses.

However, even if you prefer to handle questions after your speech, don't ever finish proceedings with answers to questions. Always give yourself enough time to end your presentation with a great summation of what you want your audience to remember, feel and do. After all, you need your audience to leave focused and energised by your talk. .

With the best will in the world, a Q&A session can put a damper on great ideas if it results in vexatious, off-point or even banal questions being raised. Even when great questions are asked:

- If they're detailed, they can move your audience's focus towards minutiae, just when you need them to think in more big picture terms.
- It may be more appropriate to handle these offline.

This isn't to suggest that you don't want to invite questions, you absolutely do. But understand that you can do a better job by choosing your moments, and regardless of when you choose to take audience questions, let them know what you're planning at the outset.

Additionally, it's also a good idea to let them know that:

- You'll be available after your session for anyone who wants to ask you any additional questions.

- You'll be happy to receive emails afterwards if you didn't get to their questions, or in case something occurs to them later, if you're willing to do this.

Both of these will be very reassuring to your audience. The former will be especially appreciated by those who aren't comfortable asking questions in front of a crowd, but who may still need or value an opportunity to get answers.

DEALING WITH OTHER VIEWPOINTS

Having come up with logical and emotional reasons people should be persuaded by your arguments, complete with evidence for what you say and content that is memorable, there is one more thing I want you to address.

No matter how wonderful your arguments may be, you will regularly encounter people in your audience who oppose some or even all of your ideas, and these audience members can be tough nuts to crack. Their views may not mesh with yours for any number of different reasons:

- Not wanting to change from how things are today (aka 'We like it the way it is' or 'Don't try to fix things that ain't broken' or 'Status quo rules')

- Concerns over the possible consequences of your ideas

- Objections to elements of your arguments, for example, price/costs, needs, priorities or other matters
- Distrust of you or your motives
- Self-interest

Regardless of why people hold views that are contrary to yours or the strength of conviction they attach to these, don't ignore them or hope they'll just go away. Take the time to research what you believe their other points of view may be, why they may believe such things, and just how much merit there is in their arguments.

Don't be afraid to delve into opposing issues. Often you'll find that you're not completely right and they're not completely wrong. Instead, there may be many shades of grey in between.

Make some lists:

- What are the opposing arguments?
- Which of these is the most important?
- Why might these be true?
- Even if not true, why would these views be held?

Understand that if you want to change people's minds, you must first appreciate where they are coming from. Also, be aware that some attitudes are more engrained than others, based on experiences or perceptions, and it can take quite some effort to encourage people to alter these.

Before we learn how to deal with objections, it might help to understand just how attitudes are changed. Commonly, people who resist change need to be brought on a journey to move from one set of thinking to another.

The following stages will be familiar to anyone who manages organisational change:

- Denial. Nothing is happening or 'I don't need to do anything'.
- Tried it, don't like it, the old way is better. This change isn't needed.
- We're trying it, but I'm not yet convinced.
- That's the way we should have been doing it in the first place (now ingrained).

Just because others may have differing views and good reasons for feeling the way they do, it doesn't mean they are right or, even if they are, that their views should hold sway. There can be other factors that should have a bearing. Sometimes satisficing or adopting the least worst option is better than maintaining the status quo.

FACTORING IN OTHER VIEWS

So how do you factor into account other people's perspectives? It depends:

- Are the other views valid?
- Are they material (do they matter)?
- Are you offering ideas that are genuinely offering more value than the status quo?

If there are good reasons why opposing views are held, you should absolutely acknowledge them.

But let's say that you encounter widespread resistance, founded on views that are flawed. You may still need to address these, even if you feel it shouldn't be necessary. No matter why people are against you, understand that the best way to overcome objections is to acknowledge them, get ahead of them and provide compelling arguments regarding why your views should hold more sway.

Don't wait to the end of a presentation to tackle other views. You are better off dealing with these early in a speech, to increase the level of attention you can command from those who are less than excited about your ideas. You'll know these and recognise them instantly: the sort who have their arms folded, just waiting for you to finish so they can say something to torpedo whatever you suggested.

Here's how to get 'ahead of the curve'. As an example, you can say something like:

'Now I understand that there are some people who may feel XXX, and they might hold these views because [give some examples], but the reality is [now start speaking to your arguments].'

This isn't meant to be a precise script, but an example of how you can start to do three really important things:

1. Tell them you understand.

2. Establish trust.

3. Pave the way for your point.

TELL THEM YOU UNDERSTAND

You are letting your audience, including those who may agree with you as well as those in other camps, know that you understand and acknowledge that there may be other points of view. Acknowledge that there are other points of view that might need to be considered.

ESTABLISH TRUST

In this situation you are likely to be seen as someone who is more trustworthy. By showing your audience that you recognise and address concerns or views that could be contrary to your arguments, you will come over as someone who is more reasonable and less truculent than speakers who don't.

PAVE THE WAY FOR YOUR POINT

You are laying the foundation for a more effective argument for two reasons:

- If your argument is sound, you will address many issues that could be raised later, when you're finished speaking, that might derail your ability to persuade people to believe you and want to take action.

- Scoring first makes it difficult for others to then stand up and argue a contrary view, especially if you've already made and dealt with their points. This is because the audience has heard reasons why they shouldn't dwell on these points and your arguments should hold more sway. You've launched a pre-emptive strike.

You are potentially doing people who may have other views, for which they may be well known, a favour. Think about this from the other person's point of view. In their shoes, if they're already known to have a particularly strong view on a given topic, they may feel under pressure to give voice to these opposing views.

And if the topic at hand is controversial or emotional – like a political matter or a decision that may cost a company, association or club a great deal of money – there's a good chance that the audience may want and need to hear contrary views before deciding what they might support.

So when you acknowledge those other views and why people may feel that way before making the arguments you propose, even if they don't agree with you at the outset, they're more likely to hear you out because you're showing that you're listening to them.

This is because:

1. People seek acknowledgment when they have concerns.

2. It helps them to rationalise why their own arguments didn't prevail.

3. It aids them to save face.

4. In any case, it eases the other guy's burden if and when they're asked, 'Well, why didn't we go down your route?'

IDEAS NOT ACTIONED

But there is a broader point in all of this. An argument, like a sales pitch, can be well received. You may sit down after putting your points over and think, 'That's the business! I think I've done enough.' Then, despite the strength of your arguments, they don't get actioned. Nothing happens. The bad news is ... it happens all the time. Why?

Unlike a sales meeting, where you can ask questions to better understand a prospective or existing client's needs, you typically won't have the opportunity to ask too many questions of any audience during your speech. Even if most of your audience seems to be on your side, buying your arguments, seeing your point of view and recognising all the benefits adopting your ideas could bring, you may still not win the day if they don't feel sufficiently inspired to do something.

All too often, it's because you actually haven't done enough. Despite making perfectly good arguments, a failure to adequately address stated or unstated objections or opposing points of view may leave your audience underwhelmed, and lacking compunction to take any action. That's not good enough.

LACK OF RETURN

The most common reason for audiences not to act in these situations is lack of return. Commonly, it comes down to not being sufficiently convinced that the price for adopting or supporting your ideas, which can include personal capital as well as time and any financial consideration, offers sufficient return. They may feel this way because you didn't do enough to pre-emptively address potential objections or roadblocks, and it's up to you to find out what these are, by doing your homework before you set to work.

COMMON OBJECTIONS

The more you know about your target audiences and what they believe, what they have tended to support in the past, what they tend to rail against and so forth, the better. Incidentally, while there may be occasions when you'll be caught off-guard by objections you weren't expecting, you'll likely find you can predict at least 90 per cent or more of what could get in the way beforehand.

Common objections are things like:

- No need
- Not a priority
- No money
- Not enough time
- Lack or resources
- Technical or operational constraints

There could be other things as well. After all, audiences and the context in which you may give your speech can vary widely, but you get the point. Don't ignore the other guys' points of views, especially if they have the capacity to derail your own argument.

UNPLANNED OR UNANSWERABLE QUESTIONS

But what do you do if you're asked a question and you haven't determined how you wish to answer it? Or maybe it's one where you don't know the answer?

First off, never be tempted to wing it! Don't try to conjure up answers or make guesses, even somewhat educated ones. You run the risk of damaging your credibility if your audience forms the view that you don't know what you're talking about or are 'trying it on'. And once you lose trust from your audience, it's never fully regained!

If you don't know the answer to a question and it has merit, acknowledge the question and whoever posed it and say how you'd like to handle it. For instance, you might say:

- 'That's a good question. I'm not in a position to answer it now/today, but can you leave it with me and I'll try to get back to you with an answer as soon as possible?'

- 'I don't know, but it sounds like something I should look into. Let's take that one offline and, depending on what I/we find out, we can come back to this later.'

These responses are not meant to placate, rather they are intended to show that:

- You are listening to your audience and focused on producing the best results for them.
- You are more concerned about facilitating better results for your audience than touting yourself as the fountain of all knowledge.

Remember, it's not about you.

CHAPTER ELEVEN

WRITING, HONING AND OWNING YOUR SPEECH

11

"If I am to speak ten minutes, I need a week for preparation; if fifteen minutes, three days; if half an hour, two days; if an hour, I am ready now"

Woodrow Wilson

Winston Churchill used to say of public speaking, 'polish until it glitters'. He was right. Your audience won't want to see you working hard, and you don't want to feel like you're making hard work of it either. While there are people who may feel that they want to appear natural, who don't want to give the impression of being over-rehearsed, it's hard to be good at anything without practice.

If you turn up at an event and 'wing it', your audience will know straightaway. Even if you've gotten away with a seat-of-the-pants approach in the past, don't use this method. You are doing a disservice to both you and your audience. So let's talk about how you can get yourself ready for a speech. From previous chapters we know there are three areas you must consider when preparing a speech:

Content (what you want to say)

- What messages you want to deliver

- What evidence you will provide to your audience to back up the points you want to make

- How you can make your arguments meaningful, memorable and actionable

- What you want your audience to believe and do when you're done

Structure (what you will use to make your arguments)

- What to include and exclude
- How to construct arguments to make them more persuasive
- How to complete your story flow

Delivery (how you will communicate with your audience)

- Words
- Body language
- Tone
- Actions
- Images

Fitting your speech comfortably to the time available to you is also an important consideration. See chapter 15 for more on time management.

WRITING AN OUTLINE

In chapter 6, we spoke of the importance of getting into the habit of developing an outline first. This should cover:

- The essential points you want to make
- Why these points are true
- What examples you can give to illustrate these points
- If there are opposing points of view, what these might be
- How you might both combat these and use the arguments to boost what you want to say

While it's possible to bypass some of these steps at this stage, experienced speakers will not. A structured approach to speech development actually will aid rather than hinder your creativity and will consistently produce more relevant and engaging talks. And for good reason; it's always easier to start a journey if you have a clear idea of where you need to go. Determine your desired destination first and then build a map to help bring your target audiences on the journey you have in mind.

POST-OUTLINE STEPS

Once you've completed your outline, here is a proven approach you can use to develop a speech.

1. Write a first draft (no editing allowed).

2. Complete several rounds of saying your speech aloud and editing as you go.

3. Reduce your speech to bullet points and practise aloud until the speech can be delivered without reference to any original notes.

4. Further hone your speech based on watching and listening to yourself delivering it in practice.

If your speech is important, you could add the following step.

5. Test drive the speech in front of trusted peers, advisers or a limited number of carefully selected audience members.

This is the process for turning your material into your final speech and involves an intermingling of edits and practising from here on in. The following is what you should do.

CREATING A FIRST DRAFT

Having decided your outline, what you want your central message to be, why it's true, how you can illustrate your points of view, and how you may tackle other viewpoints, your next step is to write a first draft of your speech in one go. Yes, really! If you have an important speech to make, this is a great way to let your thoughts start to percolate.

Write it from start to finish. Don't stop, don't edit, don't second guess – just write what comes into your head and keep going until you've covered anything you may want to say. Now, stop. Ideally put your speech away for the day, and don't look at it again until a day or more later. Here's why.

Do you remember from school days when you opened an exam paper for a subject that you struggled with? Let's say there were four or five questions that you should answer. You may well have followed the time-honoured tradition of scanning the exam paper to see what was involved in each question, making a few notes as you went along, then homing in on one or two questions that seemed easier than the others. Yes? So, do you remember what happened when you later had to answer the questions that initially appeared tougher?

Mysteriously, they often somehow seemed less daunting than when you first saw them. You aren't imagining it. This common phenomenon is down to how your brain works. While you were answering questions you found easier to do, your subconscious was working away on the other matters, rattling around on autopilot in the deep, dark recesses of your brain for any information and logic that might help to tackle those problems later.

When you write a speech and leave it overnight, you will often find that you can't help but think about the content of your speech consciously during the day and subconsciously at night. As you do, your brain will often help to assemble better ways of saying something, or come up with different angles that may not have occurred to you when first writing your speech. The upshot is that when you come to edit your speech, you are likely to find the process easier, more creative, and you'll often feel more confident in the ways you express yourself.

FURTHER EDITS AND SPEAKING ALOUD

Once fermented, go back and look at your 'first cut' speech. Read it out loud and edit it as you go. But remember do not edit without reading it aloud.

Reading aloud makes a world of difference. After all, the whole point of a speech is that you are going to say it out loud anyway, and editing it as if it were a document or a written report is the wrong way to go. You see, the way we speak is different to the way we write in many ways, including the following:

- Our sentences are shorter.
- We use less complex words.
- We are more informal in how we say things.
- We are less concerned with grammar.
- We add in more colloquial language.
- We commonly add in more dialogue.

Our spoken words will seem more natural and less stilted than written words. Now read your first correction of your speech out loud again. Edit it further, until you are happy with both what is said and how it sounds.

At this point, check your revised speech to make sure you can easily see your central message, supporting arguments, illustrations and rebuttals. Is it starting to come together? To make sense? Does it include memorable and actionable ideas? Good. Now we're on to the next stage – when you will start to hone your speech and really own it.

REDUCE YOUR SPEECH TO BULLET POINTS

Get yourself a few blank postcards, commonly called index cards, from a stationery shop and create a series of bullet points to capture your speech. Use large print and put enough space between each for easy reading. And remember to number the cards. The bullet points will ultimately serve as prompts for you to deliver your speech.

Initially, you're going to break the speech down into small, bite-sized chunks. Write a bullet point to capture the key point within each paragraph or two in as few words as possible. Limit yourself to six words or less, as if you were creating a headline for a newspaper or magazine article. Think short, snappy, to the point and clear.

Once you've done this, underline the most important word or two words in each headline and chances are you've got some pretty good prompts to include in your index card. Incidentally, this process is wonderful for forcing you to assess what you believe to be the cornerstone of each point you make, which will necessarily make it easier for you to speak to these more clearly later on.

Practice being spontaneous. Aim to sound natural, never stilted.

Practised spontaneity

There's no such thing as a great impromptu speaker. All of the best speakers throughout the ages have worked on 'practised spontaneity':

'Spontaneity is a meticulously prepared art.'
Oscar Wilde

'It usually takes me more than three weeks to prepare a good impromptu speech.'
Mark Twain

'Give me six hours to chop down a tree, and I will spend the first four hours sharpening the axe.'
Abraham Lincoln

PRACTISE ALOUD AGAIN

Once you've gone through your entire speech and have your list of bullet points, your next job is to practise your speech out loud again. I recommend that you do this on your own, standing approximately 10 to 12 feet from a corner of the room. First, let me explain why I want you to do this.

When you make a speech or presentation, there will typically be a gap between you and your audience so that everyone can see and hear you. Having this gap can create an unnatural and even unnerving experience for a speaker. You don't have regular conversations with people so far away from you, as that would feel really weird, so it's a strange situation for most people. Hence, many novice speakers will attempt to project their voice in a way that is different from how they speak normally.

Speaking in this way is not a good idea, as there's a good chance that you will sound contrived, which can be disconcerting for both you and your audience. So practising by placing yourself at a distance from a fixed point, like a corner, allows you the opportunity to get used to having your voice carry a short distance.

You'll also get used to any echoes that may happen when you speak at a live event. It offers the possibility too of mimicking how you may address each side of a room. This will be covered in detail when we get to body language in chapter 13.

WORKING FROM YOUR BULLETS

By creating bullet points that capture the essence of what you want to say for every few paragraphs, you will be sure to focus on and share these ideas with your audience. But beyond this, you will find that you will use other words – ones that come more naturally to you. You will sound like you are having more of a conversation with your audience than if you try to parrot your script verbatim.

This is good because it's unnatural when you're chatting with someone to have a precise script. You don't do that when talking with friends or colleagues, and even at meetings or more formal affairs, you may jot down a few points when you want to say something and then flesh these out with whatever words feel appropriate at that time.

As you practise your speech, you may find it useful to have the last edit of your full speech to hand as well as the bullets. This allows you to have a quick look for any bits you forget as you go. While it's fine to refer to these the first or even second time you practise your speech, try to reduce your dependency on your longhand notes with each additional practice.

Your goal will be to practise giving your speech as many times as you need in this way. At the end of doing this, you should be in a position to give your speech without reference to your full speech text and be able to rely exclusively on prompts from your bullet points.

BECOMING A NATURAL

Why are you doing this? You're becoming a natural. You're internalising your speech, becoming more familiar with the points you want to make and, crucially, you're doing something really important with the words you use. Even after your first few passes at your practice speech, you will use different words each time you speak. Great! That's exactly what you want, as you should never stick rigidly to a script.

MEMORISING WORDS

One of the things many, indeed most, of our students do at the outset of courses is try to memorise more than they should. Having written their speeches, they somehow feel obliged to follow it more strictly than they should. Working from the bullet points prevents this. Does this sound counter-intuitive? Surely if a speech is well crafted and has been edited many times, you would want to use what you've created – your best material? Well, in fact you will find that you are using it, but not in a slave-like fashion.

But you're doing even more. As you move away from memorising a speech, a number of things will happen:

- You will have the opportunity to look at your audience more, as you would your companions in a conversation.

- You'll look less strained.

Generally when we try to memorise words, we tend to do two things:

1. We speed up because we're afraid we'll forget what was in our mind. And this makes it hard for an audience to keep up with you.

2. We look uncomfortable if we struggle to remember one or more parts of our spiel.

An audience that senses you are uncomfortable will tend to share in your discomfort, which distracts from the points you want to make. Remember, like Churchill, work on practised spontaneity and if you find you can focus your audiences' attention on the central points and find many ways of expressing similar sentiments to them, you'll soon start to feel more confident. Even if a speaker has a terrific memory and nerves of steel, relying on memory to keep extracting what is to be said will cause disconnects with your audience.

This is because we commonly need to tap into the recesses of our brains to remember facts, figures and/or points we want to make. And when you do this, your audience will typically see your eyes go up or fade off into the distance as you access your memory cells instead of looking at them. The result? You look like you're uncomfortable and working too hard. Funnily enough, this will be true on both counts!

PRACTISING YOUR DELIVERY

As you practise your speech, it is always a good idea to work alone. You don't need an audience at this stage, and you certainly don't need any critics, however well-meaning your family or friends may be. Plus, the first person who needs to be persuaded about anything is you. If you find what you say believable, you're off to a good start. On the other hand, if you find that somehow you haven't yet convinced yourself, then you need to stop and reframe.

> ## To succeed as a speaker, commit to practice and preparation

If speech critiques are important to you, don't leave these to the last minute. Make sure you have enough time to recover from any unexpected observations or suggestions, make any changes you agree are needed and practise or hone the new speech properly. Don't ever leave it too late. You may be forced to do a rewrite of your speech if the following were misinterpreted by your faux audience:

- What was the main takeaway message?
- What did the images or ideas you shared with your audience mean?
- Were your examples meaningful?

These are discussed in more detail later in the chapter. Meanwhile, there are a few more useful things to do when limbering up for a big event.

STAND IN FRONT OF A MIRROR

Try giving your speech in front of a full-length mirror first. This can be quite helpful if you feel a little nervous, as you get to see what your audience sees while you're speaking – and it usually isn't that scary. If you take the opportunity to do this, look out for your facial expressions and hand movements. Do they look natural to you? If they look in any way contrived, stop and aim for something you would find more normal.

It's also a good opportunity to try out some gestures, just to see what they look like. However, I would caution against purposely injecting more gestures into a speech than you would usually use. Don't get caught out, as it can look artificial. See chapter 13 for more about body language.

LISTEN AND LEARN – RECORD YOUR VOICE

One other thing you should consider trying is a voice recorder. Since many people nowadays have smartphones, there's a good chance you already carry one whenever you go. Look up the recording function and use it, or beg, borrow or buy a cheap voice recorder. Recording how you sound can serve two very useful functions:

1. It can help you to get used to how your voice sounds.

2. It gives you the chance to listen to your tone.

HOW DO YOU SOUND?

Interestingly, many people don't like the sound of their own voice, and can even be disappointed to discover that they sound the way they do. It doesn't sound the same as it does 'in your head' when you are speaking. But knowing how you sound can be quite comforting, if it means you can stop worrying about what others hear while you actually perform. It's good reassurance.

We'll come back to this later in chapter 14, as your voice is part of who you are, so being comfortable with it is a good start.

DO YOU SOUND LIKE YOU CARE?

Audiences will use your tone to judge your conviction and sincerity. So when you listen to yourself, don't spend too much time critiquing your actual speech. Focus instead on whether you would believe that person if you were listening to a stranger. Does your voice come over as that of an honest person? Do you sound like you care about the topic?

> Consider recording your talk. Be passionate and earnest. If you sound like you care, your audience will also.

You can learn a great deal from audio recordings, and I encourage you to listen to yourself on a regular basis. It can help you to focus on how passionate and earnest you sound, and if you can believe in yourself, there's a good chance others may do too. But if you hear yourself and you're not convinced, you need to make some changes.

LIMBERING UP WITH LIVE AUDIENCES

If it's a really big speech, and you need to make sure that it will work, then running it past a trusted mentor, speech coach or peer who is typical of your audience could be helpful. Steer away from well-meaning critics like family and friends who are not your target audience.

Also, beware of leaving this to the eleventh hour. You could find yourself with virtually no time to start again and get sufficient practice in. Worse, when you wrote and honed your speech, you had a level of confidence that what you said made sense, captured what you wanted to say, and would encourage people to feel a certain way. That confidence may now be shot down in flames.

If your audience feedback suggests that a big makeover is needed, you could find your confidence undermined. So here's a tip – if speech critiques are important to you, don't leave these to the last minute.

CHAPTER TWELVE

ACTIVELY ENGAGING WITH YOUR AUDIENCE

"A dream becomes a goal when action is taken towards its achievement."

Bo Bennett

12

There's another vital job you must complete while getting ready for your presentation. You will need to gear your audience up to take actions after you speak.

Although, speaking to others on a one-to-many basis can feel somewhat passive, since you're the one doing most of the talking, you need your audience to become sufficiently engaged and inspired by your talks to put your arguments into practice. You must never think of public speaking as a one-way street. If it is, no value will have been realised and your efforts will have served no purpose.

SELL THE BENEFITS

Start the process of getting your audiences excited by your ideas, internalising them and acting upon them as quickly as you can. Within certain limitations, audience interaction can act as a vital means to get the ball rolling.

Remember it's in your vested interest to make sure there is perceived benefit in what you ask people to do, and the more the better. When planning for interaction, always answer the 'what's in it for me' question for audience members, no matter what you ask of them. Why is it worth their while? What role should the exercise you suggest play in the journey you want your audience to undertake?

Also don't surprise your audience if you need them to actively participate in your presentation. They should never feel ambushed or worried about the prospect of being embarrassed in front of others. Let them know upfront that you'll be asking them to get involved and reassure them that you appreciate any help they can give you, as it will be of benefit to all of the attendees.

> Start the process of getting your
> audience excited about your ideas,
> internalizing them and acting upon
> them as soon as you can.

HOW TO WIN HEARTS AND MINDS

Before looking at the different interaction methods you
might use, be aware that when asking people to do
something new, you may have to work on their attitudes as
well as behaviours to win hearts and minds.

ATTITUDES

Our attitudes tend to be relatively engrained. They are
typically based on what you believe, which is formed from:

- A combination of your experiences
- What you have been exposed to over time
- Perceptions

Surprising as it may seem, many of our attitudes are based
on things that we believe simply because others have told
or convinced us they are true. And the thing about attitudes
is that they tend to be much more ingrained than our
behaviours. This is hardly surprising, when you think about it,
as we accumulate them over many years.

Research shows that our core attitudes can be set as early as
the age of six, and influence how we react to events around
us from then on. They do of course change as we modify our
views of the world and our environments; however, we may
need to experience or become aware of something new or
contrary to our beliefs many times before we change our
attitudes.

Of all the vehicles used to change our attitudes, beyond those we redirect through behaviour, we are especially influenced by the media we encounter. Our views on matters we don't deal with on a daily basis, or on topics that only concern us in a broader sense, such as international events, politics and national news, are commonly shaped by the media we see or hear.

So if we only read a select number of newspapers, or only tune into a limited number of television or radio news sources, our views on all these things may be sculpted by the media producers in question, and their views or slants on events. Naturally, these views too are built on whatever we perceive from our personal experiences.

WHY DOES THIS MATTER TO A SPEAKER?

It has to do with context, what your audience believes and why. If your goal is to change attitudes, then you need to understand what people perceive before you seek to alter their beliefs. You need to understand that it may take some time and effort to help people accept and then adopt new attitudes. Much of your effort will need to be devoted to encouraging your audiences to feel it's in their best interest to try something once or many times, as a means of helping them to acquire new frames of reference.

BEHAVIOUR

It's much easier to change behaviours than attitudes. Marketers will tell you that to encourage custom from people who don't buy or use their products, one of the first things they want to do is to encourage them to take a 'trial'. Once people have done something at least once, there is a far higher chance they'll be prepared to do it a second time, and so on.

After all, if you've tried something, you have a basis for determining what you got out of the experience. If you keep experiencing something, there's a good chance your views regarding that activity will become more fixed, commonly leading to engrained attitudes.

TECHNIQUES TO ACHIEVE INTERACTION

Used correctly, interaction techniques can help your audiences to visualise how your ideas apply to them and are valuable, relying more on 'show' versus 'tell' methods in the process. As you consider the role interaction should play in the journey you'd like your audiences to take (during as opposed to after your talk), make sure anything you ask them to do:

- complements and supports the ideas you want them to action after the event, and
- can be easily completed within the time available to you when speaking
- is realistic
- is simple and not too time consuming
- is (or at least seems) easy to accomplish
- is demonstrably worthwhile.

Delayed gratification is always a harder sell, so try to frontload the perceived benefit of any suggested actions.

STRIKE WHILE THE IRON IS HOT

When considering forms of interaction you may use, bear in mind that it may only help you to address part of the journey you want your audience to take. You'll still need them to commit to action after you've spoken. To this end, don't let any grass grow under your feet. Try to encourage immediate action.

If your audience doesn't feel something needs to be done straightaway, there's a good chance other demands for their attention or priorities will emerge in the following days or weeks that will get in the way of auctioning your ideas. So strike while the iron is hot! In an era of monumental information overload and overscheduling, eaten bread is soon forgotten.

THE BEST FORMS OF INTERACTION

While there are no hard and fast rules on this, I recommend you consider combining a bottom-up with a top-down approach to pitch your interaction at an appropriate level for your audience.

- Try starting with what you want the end result of your presentation to be. What do you want your audience to believe and/or do once you're done?

- Now consider where your audience is starting from. What are your assumptions about what they know, believe or care about?

- Think visual, and think experience. What pictures and experiences might help your audience on their journey to being persuaded (from their viewpoints) about your ideas?

Boost audience engagement through a combination of stories, questions, demonstrations and/or exercises.

TYPES OF INTERACTION TECHNIQUES

Depending on what you need to achieve, some of the more important interaction techniques you should consider include:

1. Storytelling

2. Questions

3. Demonstration

4. Exercises

Storytelling

Have you noticed the stories scattered throughout this book? I use them to make points come alive and hopefully entertain you. Although it may appear more passive than other methods, storytelling is a marvellous way to help audiences truly engage in what you say. As you will have gathered from chapter 8, we're all storytellers. We read, watch television and movies – stories are all around us and, fact or fiction, they are a familiar way to gain information from another party. As audience members find themselves immersed in a story, the characters and how your tales may have personal applications to them tend to come to life.

Stories can help your audience visualise how things could be. For examples of how to use this method with great effect, look no further than Steve Jobs, who was one of the best exponents of this 'show and tell' method of audience engagement.

Steve understood that audiences remember more of things they can see or imagine, and he spent most of his time on stage when promoting new products illustrating how people could 'now do something'. His aspirational 'now you can' messages were tied into meaningful images that were literally worth thousands of words and more.

Aspirational messages

Steve Jobs was leveraging something that has been known to work in advertising circles for a long time. Audiences consistently prefer to be depicted as they would wish to be seen ahead of how they actually are.

When making hundreds of commercials for different ethnic groups in America in the early 1990s, I witnessed this truth myself, again and again. Showing an audience succeeding by doing something new always produced better results that showing the same audiences in ways they perceived to be in a less positive light. And the reason for this is simple. No one likes to be associated with failings.

That's why straight (exaggeration-free) aspirational messages will beat other messages time and again. They evoke more powerful, emotional responses.

HOW STORYTELLING WORKS

We basically believe what we can see. Being told something without seeing it requires faith, and while that can work too where people trust you, a visual demo is much more powerful.

Bear in mind that the real people who need to be convinced about something may not be in the room when you speak to an audience, so you may require your audience to form part of your 'persuasion committee' when they go back home and put your case to others. If they have seen something and believe it does what you say it does, as a consequence they will be far better able to describe in their own words what they've seen and how they feel about it to others.

Questions

In their 2007 book, Made to Stick, Chip and Dan Heath spoke of six principles of ideas that gain traction and that work time and again. Indeed all of these notions could have been drawn directly from a classical art of rhetoric playbook, so this is not something newfangled in any way. Here's what they found.

In addition to the importance of simple messages, evocative stories and tapping into emotional appeals, they also found ideas that endure tended to:

- Engage curiosity and interest, by opening gaps in knowledge and helping to close them.

- Offer concrete benefits which are capable of being 'seen in action'.

- Be ideas that carry their own credentials, i.e. they are capable of being self-evidencing.

Engaging questions that are both on point and appropriate to your audience and the circumstances in which you need to operate can be a terrific means to many of these ends. Questions necessarily require two-way communication, and they usually result in audience members paying greater attention than when they merely listen to a speaker talking. They can be used for a host of reasons, including to:

- Validate and even quantify what an audience does or has done in the past (historic behaviour) or what they know, believe and/or value.

- Remind audiences of things that may not have been top of mind but which you wish to dig out as they will matter to your arguments.

- Encourage reactions to ideas that are new and/or could require change from the audience.

- Involve audience members individually or collectively in determining how an idea could be put into effect, what this might require (in time, money, other resource and effort terms) and the likely payoff for doing so.

Interestingly, audiences will typically compare perceived benefits from the latter with what they believe to be their next best alternative. But here's a caveat, all too often this will be a default position of doing nothing or making no change.

So there are many reasons why adding select questions into a presentation can help to more fully engage your audience. But I also want to add a note of caution. Beware of injecting leading or rhetorical questions into proceedings. For example:

- 'Isn't it true that...?'
- 'Aren't you glad you don't...?'

While they aren't a complete no-no, these questions can be perceived as being manipulative or controlling, and if you're dealing with emotive or challenging issues, you run the risk of damaging your credibility and therefore your persuasiveness.

AUDIENCE INVOLVEMENT

If you'd like to use current or historic audience knowledge or experience to support or validate what you want to say at an event, it's worth considering getting some or all of your event attendees involved in what you're doing before you say a word. For instance:

- Perhaps you can solicit views about your topic or arguments from key audience members or influencers, and share their views with your audience.

- Perhaps you could ask participants to answer some questions before you speak, for example, about key concerns, experiences or issues, and then find ways to use these findings to make more compelling arguments.

Where practical, the use of pre-emptive homework can hugely increase audience engagement if it is used to speak more accurately to the problems they face, addressing these and why people should care.

Audience involvement and need for simplicity

The movie *An Inconvenient Truth* was released in 2006 and made it into the top ten grossing documentary movies produced in the United States until 2010. Directed by **Davis Guggenheim**, it kick-started international awareness of the messages **Al Gore** was championing to 'make the issue of global warming a recognized problem worldwide'.

It was to have a transformative effect: moving so many cinema-goers around the world from a point of ignorance or apathy about the melting Polar ice caps, the extent to which the ozone layer has been damaged, the real-life examples of the ravages of global warming, and more. It moved many audience members from perceptions, little of which were based on experiences, to a realisation that the world has some serious issues that need to be addressed right now. And this wasn't just a green issue; it was also an urgent global social and economic issue that required worldwide, joint-up action.

But here's the point. Even though the messages delivered through this movie version of a speech Al Gore had given many times before had tremendous impact, implementation of many of the changes cited as necessary has been slow to date. Perhaps the effect of this campaign might have been greater if it was tied into a series of simple things the audiences could put into effect straightaway.

Demonstration

If your topic lends itself to demonstration, great. This is where your audience can try your ideas out, see what they think and maybe even share their thoughts about their experiences. Sell the sizzle! You'll create a more emotionally engaging experience for all and sundry in the process. Of course, you don't necessarily have to have every member of the audience involved. You could ask for volunteers to participate and help you illustrate the points you want to make.

Finding ways to let audience members experience and see ideas in action applies to any form of speaking. Simply put, get to action as quickly as you can. It categorically speaks louder than words and is more persuasive.

Actions speak louder than words

A number of years ago, I saw the Irish golfer Padraig Harrington, who had just won the British Open for the first time, give a golf clinic to a group of youngsters. He had the audience in the palm of his hand as he enthusiastically described and demonstrated the secrets he had learned the previous year that were allowing him to hit the ball further, despite losing a little flexibility as he became older.

But no matter how fascinating his tips were, without putting his ideas into practice quickly, most people in his audience (myself included) would forget most of his advice long before playing their next game of golf.

But then he switched gears from the long game to the short and described how, under a great deal of pressure, he played a championship-saving 40-yard pitch shot across the infamous Barry Burn in front of the 18th green at Carnoustie, which stopped just 4 feet away from the pin. He was to hole that putt en route to winning that day.

However, this time he invited two of the juniors to try out his method. Each had a go and each saw that the shot worked perfectly at once. Then they both tried it again a few more times and every shot they hit was just as good as their first efforts.

They were convinced immediately by seeing they could put his ideas into practice and play a shot that most amateurs could not. And I can attest that the ideas stuck, as I still see the same duo making regular use of what I call the 'Harrington Special' all these years later.

Exercises

Beyond storytelling, asking questions and demonstrations, there are times when it can be really helpful to put your audience members to work. This is especially true if you want to enlist help from participants in determining how to give effect to ideas. These exercises can vary but here are some examples:

- Asking individuals or groups to write things down

- Brainstorming on specific topics

- Trying things out

- Tackling sample issues or case studies

- Sharing reactions, observations or conclusions

Needless to say, if you're going to ask people to do things, you need to be reasonably confident about the likely outcome, which should support and not undermine arguments you want your audience to adopt.

The upside to asking people to do meaningful things in groups (smaller tend to be better and more intimate) is that it affords you the opportunity to foster teamwork, while bolstering potential buy-in to your ideas. Let me explain why this matters. Audience engagement and buy-in will increase if they can 'show' themselves or each other why there's merit in your ideas rather than relying largely on passive acceptance of your arguments and repeating what you said to others.

CHAPTER THIRTEEN

THE POWER OF BODY LANGUAGE

"Men trust their
ears less than
their eyes."

Herodotus

Audiences notice quite a few things, but in terms of body language, let's focus on four of the most important of these:

1. Eye contact

2. Stance

3. Gestures

4. Managing barriers (especially, the dreaded podium)

MAKE GOOD EYE CONTACT

When having a conversation with anyone, you usually look at the person you are speaking to, and they do the same to you. It wouldn't dawn on us not to do this. If you speak to someone while looking elsewhere, it doesn't convey interest and attention. How would you react to someone who behaved that way? You'd be hard pressed not to become irritated, perhaps?

Most of us expect others to look at us when we're speaking with them. If they don't, we're likely to think along the lines of 'that obnoxious so-and-so isn't listening to me,' and become annoyed by behaviour that would ordinarily be deemed very rude.

Yet, when it comes to speaking in public, it's remarkable how many speakers don't follow the standard rules of communication. Maybe it's because speaking to many rather than one or a few people doesn't feel like a regular conversation. It can seem more a form of one-way communication, almost like a broadcast or even a lecture. It can seem as if the rules of engagement are different.

Intuitively, it may feel like you can't look at an audience in the same way you would one or two people during a conversation. After all, how can you look at 20 to 50 or even many hundreds of people at the same time?

I'll get to that in a moment – but first, here's an absolute: if you fail to look at your audience, you will struggle to gain their engagement. Your audience will always consciously and subconsciously pay attention to your eyes, when assessing whether they want to listen to you or care about what you say.

That said, let's acknowledge the obvious issues you need to overcome:

- Presenting to a group is not equivalent to having a regular conversation.
- You can't look at everyone all the time if you have many people in a room.

BAD TIPS

Obviously, looking at the general direction of your audience is important, but here are a few daft ideas about how to do this that have been bandied about as 'helpful advice' for speakers. Please ignore them!

- **Imagine that your audience is naked!**

  Really? Could it be that imaging your audience in a ridiculous state will somehow make them seem less fierce, or that you'll find the situation almost amusing? Do you really believe this will make you more relaxed? Do you know anyone who regularly uses this technique with any success? Of course not, and for good reason, it's nonsense! Even if you could imagine such things for a few seconds, could you do it for a sustained period, say 5 minutes, never mind 20 or 30 minutes? Enough said.

- **Looking past or over your audience's heads.**

  The idea here is that the method encourages audience members to think you're looking at them, even though you're not. While technically possible to do, it would be exhausting to keep going for any length of time. Plus, it simply won't allow a speaker the opportunity to cement the connections he or she needs with individual audience members throughout a speech.

  Forget these avoidance techniques.

TECHNIQUES FOR GOOD EYE CONTACT

So here's what you do need to do, and why:

- **Don't have favourites.**

  You can but you shouldn't look at the same people for the duration of your speech. Instead, your goal should be to engage pretty much every audience member on a reasonably frequent basis during the course of your presentation. This is quite easy really, in that you don't need to (and nor should you) dwell on any individual for longer than a few seconds at a time. Moving past the fact that you'll likely freak people out if you stare at them for too long, all you need to do is to look right to left and back to front of your audience gradually, and over the course of your speech.

- **Catch the fish that nibble.**

  As you scan the audience like this, you'll find you naturally catch some people's eyes. Take the time to nod or smile at them, thus sprinkling your attention over different members of the audience.

As you do this, you'll notice something very important; your audience members will naturally tend to reflect your behaviour. When you're having a conversation with someone and they nod towards you as they speak, what do you find yourself doing without thinking about it? You nod back, right? Why?

It's because you're showing the other person that you are both listening and understand what they are saying. We're all pretty much pre-programmed to do this. So at a presentation if a speaker looks at you and nods, you'll find yourself hard pressed not to nod back towards the speaker, unless you disagree with, dislike or purposely hold back from him or her.

....

• **Watch the ripples spread.**

Not only will audience members reflect back what they see you do, there's more. In most cases, the people to their left and right will tend to follow suit. This is because we all have peripheral vision, albeit a little broader for women than men. So when someone beside you nods, you'll instinctively mimic their behaviour. Next thing you know, you'll see a cascade effect, and this is really important, since people who nod at you as in a regular conversation are likely to listen more attentively than those who don't. It's a rule of conversation – a norm!

So the eyes really do have it. If you want to involve your audience, getting them to believe you care about them and pay more attention to you, you must look at them. If you fail to do this, your audience is under no obligation to look at you. And that means they don't have to (and won't) pay attention to what you say, and they will remember next to nothing.

> Frequent, good eye contact with your audience will earn you rapt attention. Without it, expect them to switch off.

STANCE – POSTURE AND MOVEMENT

The importance of posture and movement cannot be underestimated and are very noticeable to audiences.

POSTURE

Most of us don't give much thought to how we stand. But when you're audience facing, this can greatly affect how people perceive you. When we don't feel comfortable, our body language can give us away.

A surprisingly high number of people are slouchers. We let our shoulders slump, and if this is in any way pronounced, it makes you look awkward to your audience. It also suggests to them that you are ill at ease – and often they're right.

Have you ever noticed how a confident person tends to walk into a room? They look like they belong there, with purpose. They walk tall and other people in the room just seem to gravitate imperceptibly towards them. This isn't a trick or contrivance. Standing without slouching at your full height will instantly make you appear more confident in yourself, even though you may actually be a bit of a duck, calm on the surface of water and paddling like hell underneath.

But you need to avoid the appearance of looking like a board too. You don't want to be so stiff that you look like a character from Thunderbirds and incapable of action! Looking stiff will make you look just as bad as slouching.

So, we're looking for a stance that is comfortably standing to your full height with your shoulders straight as opposed to leaning forwards or slightly backwards. It's not a hard thing to do. But that's only part of what you want to achieve through your stance. You also need to reduce unnecessary movement when speaking.

MOVEMENT

The only bits you want to regularly move when speaking, unless emphasising or showing something to an audience, are your eyes and your hands. Your eyes should be looking at your audience, while your hands or gestures should draw your audience into what you say.

When repeated, any other movements can move from simple distraction to being a constant source of irritation for audiences, causing them to pay more attention to what you're doing instead of what you're saying. A speaker who moves about a lot during a speech can distract audiences from their message. Have you ever seen the actor Jim Carrey at his most animated? Many people who see him remember his way of moving more than what he says.

We all move a bit when we talk with others. But excessive movement can be distracting and typically comes from:

- Pacing as we speak (the lion)
- Rocking backwards and forwards or from side to side (the parrot)
- Folding and unfolding legs (the spider)
- Swaying (the giraffe)

Unless you are moving for effect, where you want to emphasise or illustrate something, you don't want to have too much movement going on. At the same time, you need to avoid looking stiff or stilted.

The cure for unwanted movements is really quite straightforward. Simply adopt a stance that's exactly like that which a golfer would take to play an iron shot, minus the flexing of the knees! Stand with your feet shoulder width apart, and that's all there is to it. This looks entirely comfortable, and it allows you to keep the lower part of your body relatively still as you speak, with virtually no effort.

In chapter 11, I advocated practising your speech in front of a full-length mirror when first honing your skills as a speaker. This is a good example of an area where a mirror can help; it can eradicate movements you may be unaware of until you see them in action. Giving talks to yourself while looking in the mirror is helpful so you can literally see what others see when you talk to them.

Don't worry too much about the content of your speeches as you do this; that's not what you're looking for. Your only question is 'would I believe that person?' Do you look genuine, and do your gestures look natural? In most cases the answer will be yes, because in the real world you use gestures unconsciously in conversation.

APPROPRIATE GESTURES

This is an interesting area because many people believe that they need to do more with their hands or gestures than is necessary. There are three common reasons we should use gestures:

1. To invite your audience into your speech (adding connectivity)

2. To emphasise points

3. To add description

Before we get into what works, one thing you must never do is to use contrived gestures. Your audience will notice and this can seriously undermine how much trust people place in you. No one likes to feel they are being manipulated, and faux gestures can give exactly that impression.

Used appropriately, gestures can help your audience to pay attention to what is being said and get more out of it. Great writers on rhetoric like Cicero and Quintilian were huge advocates of gestures, by which they mostly meant facial expressions and hands, and the role they play in engaging audiences, sometimes even replacing as well as complementing the words shared.

When you speak, as previously noted, it may seem to you that you're engaged in one-way communication, where you talk and your audience listens. But that's not what you want. The last thing you need is for your audience to be passive; you want them to feel they have an active role in proceedings. They should feel engaged and vitally involved in whatever you do.

OPEN HAND GESTURES

What do you think when you see someone at a meeting making an open hand gesture to you? What does it mean to you? Commonly we think, 'well, I guess he or she wants to hear what I have to say' or 'maybe they want to shake my hand?' In any case, we tend to perceive open hand gestures in positive and inviting terms. They suggest that the person making them is interested in his or her audience.

Consciously and subconsciously, we interpret this behaviour to mean that the speaker is listening to us or wants to be our friend. It's an inclusive form of behaviour. As a speaker, open hand gestures are top of the list (after eyes) as a way to let your audience know that you value them, and you want them to be part of what you are doing and saying.

Open hand gestures can be used to invite audiences in to what you say, to emphasise points and to describe various things, and most of these will occur naturally. But remember don't point your finger at anyone. For most people, it means being singled out and not always in a good way. In a one-to-many communication, people who are singled out by pointing may become uncomfortable if they feel they are the centre of attention.

EXAGGERATED GESTURES

There are some exceptions when it comes to physically showing your audience what is happening while telling stories. Stories are necessarily more animated, and as Doug Stevenson puts it in his book, Story Theater Method, you can use small gestures to describe most points but should use larger gestures for comedy.

The latter is fascinating, as so much of what makes us laugh is physical and based on exaggeration. In these circumstances, your audience knows that you're not being serious with them, and they won't judge you harshly if they think you're being contrived – because you are, in the interests of spinning a good yarn!

There are other times when you will need to consciously make your gestures somewhat bigger. This happens when you speak to larger audiences. Here's the general rule.

- If you have small audiences, keep your gestures small. In most cases we won't have to think about these, as they're no different from gestures we use in conversation with others.

- If you have a medium-sized audience – say 50 to 150 – make your gestures a little bigger, so people in the back of the room can see what you're doing. Some speaking professionals suggest that these should be more from the elbow than your wrist, but that's overthinking things. Really, you just want to include your audience in what you're saying, and your gestures need to be large enough to be seen. Just don't overdo this, and make sure gestures never look scripted. You want natural.

- If you're doing a huge gig with hundreds or even thousands of attendees, or even speaking in a stadium, go as big you can. Small gestures simply won't be seen.

BARRIERS – TO USE THE PODIUM OR NOT

If most of your presenting is done for in-house audiences, you'll likely never have to think about this question. After all, how many companies have podiums or lecterns in their conference or meeting rooms? Not many. However, if you're called upon to speak at seminars, workshops or other corporate events, you'll often face the question of whether or how you make use of a podium.

Some speakers wouldn't dare to leave the podium, and they will stand four-square behind it for entire speeches. Others find them restrictive and prefer to operate without them. To a certain extent, it's a matter of preference. There is little doubt that being able to stand closer to your audience can make for a more intimate experience for all. But not every speaker is comfortable with being in this situation, and some even find the idea intimidating.

There are of course halfway house approaches, where the speaker might use a small table in the centre of a room that they can get back to easily to refer to notes. This creates an opportunity for greater intimacy between speaker and audience, and glancing occasionally at your notes in this way won't even be noticed. As I say, it's a matter of choice.

If speaking with a podium, the only thing you should keep there are notes

HOW TO USE A PODIUM TO GOOD EFFECT

If you do use a podium, here's some advice you should follow.

• **Avoid the death grip.**

Nervous speakers commonly grip either side of the podium – please don't do this. Even if an audience can't quite see the colour in your veins, if you happen to be clinging onto it for dear life it will only make you look ill at ease. And as I've mentioned before, if you seem in any way uncomfortable, your audience will pick this up and share in your discomfort.

• **Don't limit yourself.**

More importantly, holding a podium deprives you of the opportunity to invite your audience into what you say with your gestures.

• **Use, don't abuse.**

Take a different approach. The only things you should put on a podium are your notes. Then make sure you step back a little from it, so your audience can easily see both your eyes and your hands. Use the podium as an aid, not a barrier.

You can also decide to mix it up a bit, choosing to get amongst your audience for interactive parts of your presentation, and then returning to a more central point in front of or behind a podium at other times. If you're not sure about your preferences, experiment in practice and during smaller or shorter speaking sorties.

See chapter 16 for more about venue and means of delivery.

CHAPTER FOURTEEN

TONE, ACCENTS AND HOW YOU SOUND

"Man is only great when he acts from the passions."

Herodotus

14

WHAT PEOPLE REALLY HEAR

It's an extraordinary thing, but we don't hear how we sound most of the time! When we do get to hear recordings of our voices, especially the first time, we are often surprised by how we sound. It can be like an out-of-body experience for some, and even a little uncomfortable; 'surely I don't sound like that' comes to mind.

Over the years, I've lost count of the number of clients who have told me that they don't like the sound of their own voice. Sometimes they're not excited by their accents, and at other times it has more to do with intonations or use of language. Truthfully, we can be our own worst critics!

TONE

In reality, other people are entirely used to how we sound and give it far less thought than you, the owner, may do. But there is something in your voice that audiences will always pay close attention to – your tone.

After body language, tone is the next most important tool we tend to use when assessing others and what they say. Consciously and subconsciously we listen to tone to determine what's really being said. After all, the same words can have hugely different meanings depending on how you say something.

EMPHASIS

For example, suppose I use the sentence, 'what do you do?' It's a simple question. But just see, and hear in your head, what happens if I change the tone in a short sentence by giving more emphasis to one word versus another.

- What do you do?

- **What** do you do?

- What **do** you do?

- What do **you** do?

- What do you **do**?

It changes the meaning entirely, doesn't it? As you can see, altering even small elements of what we say can cause your audience to gather entirely different meanings. They can assess whether you're:

- Calm or angry

- Happy or sad

- Emotional or stoic

- Honest or deceptive, etc.

Certainly, you may vary your emphasis from time to time to help your audience pay special attention to what you want them to consider, understand or do. This is why practising how you say things can really help you convey the sentiment you want your audience to capture.

Without practice, members of the 'Winging It Club' may manage to more or less convey what they want to say, but they are far more likely to struggle to convey anywhere near the same meaning (and therefore impact) as those who choose to hone their speeches.

However, this is only true if you have developed and nurtured a natural style, one that both suits you and works well with the material you want to share for the audience and their needs. However, that's only part of the story.

PASSION

The other element that you need to inject into your tone, if it's not already there, is passion. For those who follow my blog, you'll be familiar with one of my mantras:

'Passion counts. If you don't care, neither will your audience!'

As you now know, logic is essential in any argument you create, since what you say must make sense for an audience to 'get' what you're talking about. But emotion is also vitally important in your quest to have an audience feel something. An audience that doesn't feel strongly about something is:

- Unlikely to attach any priority to it
- Probably not going to make an effort to remember it
- Even less likely to do something about it afterwards

In addition to noticing your body language, your audience will pick up on how passionate you are about your topic, and what you want them to get from your speeches.

If you think back to speeches you found memorable, chances are you could see and hear how much the speakers seemed to care about the topic in question, and the effort they made to share their enthusiasm with you. Moving beyond the wave of excitement that Barack Obama created in the run-up to and immediate aftermath of his bid for the presidency of the United States in 2008, one of the greatest modern exponents of passion was President Ronald Reagan.

Notwithstanding that he leveraged his years of experience as a movie actor, when you listen to Ronald Reagan speak, you can't help but be drawn into his warmth and conviction. You have little doubt that he believed every word that he said, that he cared and was genuinely concerned to share every word he uttered with his audience. Someone once described his style as like spending time with your grandfather, who was passing on his worldly wisdom to you.

While there are no recordings of how he sounded as a speaker, those who heard Abraham Lincoln were frequently struck by his high, even shrill, pitch and the awkwardness of his movements when he began to deliver his speeches.

But by the time he was 10 or more minutes into his speech, few noticed these things. Instead, they were far more struck by his combination of logic, stories, humour and common or folksy language. He built up passion and didn't let go. And the result was he could keep his audiences at the edges of their seats for hours at a time. So do remember to speak with passion.

SINCERITY

While some people may have the capacity to argue that blue is red with a straight face, it's hard for most of us to fake sincerity for any length of time. Even if you utter words you don't believe with gusto and as much pathos as you can muster, there's a good chance that your audience will pick up on your little (or big) 'tells'.

Be assured, if your audiences finally start feeling you've been less than honest or sincere with them, your integrity or credibility will be dented. And that's bad news, because it's always an uphill struggle to win people back to placing trust in you if they have to spend time or energy deciding if they should believe you again this time.

STICK WITH YOUR NATURAL STYLE?

So let's look at how you sound versus just your conviction. As we've learned, speaking in public is not like having a regular conversation, and many people are less than excited by how they think they sound. I'll develop this point further when talking about accents in a moment. But what about speaking styles? Do you need to develop one as you learn the ancient art of speech making?

The answer is no, at least not in the sense that you should acquire a new way of speaking or holding court in order to engage an audience. It's more about fitting how you already speak into a slightly different environment.

Leaving aside any misgivings you may have about how you sound in general, one of the things you may become conscious of when speaking to audiences is the different sound that occurs when your voice has to carry a longer distance to reach the listeners. For one thing, you'll likely have at least two and sometimes even four plus yards between you and the front row of an audience, depending on numbers attending your speech and the set-up at the venue. That's a sharp contrast to chatting with others where you're rarely more than a yard away, so it can feel very weird.

In addition to this, whether you're with or without a microphone, you may hear something else you don't have to contend with in regular conversations – an echo. Faced with an echo, there can be a natural but misguided tendency to alter our sound, making it louder or what we perceive to be clearer. That makes us appear as if we are trying to become something of an 'Act-orrr'!

YOU ARE NOT AN ACTOR

Acting or performing is rarely a good idea for three reasons:

· **It's difficult!**

   Have you ever noticed that even real actors can struggle to maintain a false accent over the course of an entire movie or play? Even if you have a good ear for accents, it's difficult to do without a good deal of practice, and done badly, projecting an accent that is clearly not yours can be very annoying.

- **It will come over as being contrived.**

  Tied into the last point, if you try to use an accent or voice that is clearly affected, your audience will pick up on this and are likely to react badly to it. After all, how do you react when you encounter someone who you think sounds like they're trying to assume airs and graces? Do you trust that person?

  Even if you like much of what they say, there's still a good chance that you may discount or even dismiss what you hear. It's easy to assume they are attempting to be someone or something they are not. It's like you have an internal alarm system that says, 'This person doesn't sound normal – warning!' As I've said before, never trade on perceived credibility.

- **We don't feel comfortable.**

  In fact, there's a broader reason why you shouldn't assume an unnatural speaking voice; it's likely to seem weird and out of kilter to you. Yet again, this may cause you to feel uncomfortable, and if you feel out of sorts? Yep, you guessed it, audiences will tend to pick up on this and feel uncomfortable with you!

YOUR ACCENT IS PART OF WHO YOU ARE

But what happens if you have a strong accent and you're worried audiences may not understand you? Or even that they may dislike you or what you say, because of your accent? You may feel that the way you sound could attract a certain level of bias. This is a very common concern on our courses, and my answer is always the same:

> 'Dance with the girl you brought, but be prepared to have a few dancing lessons where needed.'

What do I mean? I mean that while accents can certainly present communication problems, be very careful about trying to change them. It could be counterproductive. Building on the notion that it's difficult to sustain a tone or voice that isn't natural to you for a large amount of time, there's a broader question: why would you try? Your accent is part of who you are. It goes beyond mere pronunciations and includes the inflections, tones and words or phrases you use to express your ideas. It is part of your personality.

If you try to change it, as noted previously, you run the risk that people may find your voice affected or contrived. This is especially true if audience members know you and have heard you speaking on other occasions. And, as a speaker, this can have a disastrous effect on your perceived credibility and, therefore, the value people are prepared to attach to what you say.

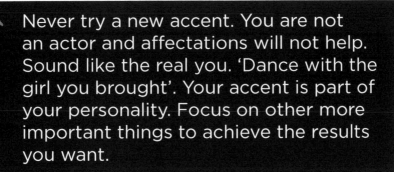

Never try a new accent. You are not an actor and affectations will not help. Sound like the real you. 'Dance with the girl you brought'. Your accent is part of your personality. Focus on other more important things to achieve the results you want.

The truth is that there are far more important factors that will influence an audience's reaction to a speaker than his or her accent. In other words, we're back to my point about the audience being much more concerned with WIIFM than how you sound.

But if you do have a strong accent, remember I did mention the possibility of dancing lessons! There are things you can do to help your audience that don't involve you acting or putting on an accent. These include pausing, your pace of speaking, your tone, and your passion. We've already looked at tone and passion, so let's focus on pausing and speaking slowly.

PAUSING

Pausing will help you avoid any sense of rushing your speech. By injecting short pauses at the end of your sentences, you will necessarily tend to achieve two things:

- You will give your audience the time and ability they need to keep pace with what you say – in essence, to hear you.

- Your audience will hear more emotion, as your tone will naturally become more modulated. And passion counts when it comes to swaying audiences to feel interested and excited about anything.

SLOW DOWN FOR GREATER IMPACT

Remember that while it is technically possible to utter 250 words a minute like auctioneers, most of us manage to speak between 120 and 160 words a minute in conversations. So don't cram this many words in when addressing an audience.

Research shows that unlike when you chat with others in a two-way dialogue, it's harder to pay attention when passively listening to a speech. That's hardly surprising, as no-one is checking in with you every few seconds to see if you're following along. Audiences connect with and recall more of what is said at a presentation when a speaker can slow down to about 80 per cent of normal conversation speed.

World-class speakers will speak even slower than this. For instance, if you watched a Nelson Mandela speech, notice how much audience engagement he achieved by slowing down to just 75 to 90 words a minute. His audiences loved it. They hear every word he said and the passion with which he uttered them. His use of pausing was just wonderful, giving his audience the time they needed to be drawn into and captivated by his ideas and offered him more time to interact with them. And that's a winning combination.

So, on the dance lesson front, focus more on content, emotion and delivery than any idea that there are good and bad accents. The consequences of appearing to behave in a contrived way are almost never worth the price of admission.

ADJUST THE VOLUME

What about volume control? Some people have soft voices, others create a more booming sound, and then there are any number of shades in between. The right volume for you to apply when speaking is usually the level you use when having conversations with others. You will rarely need to raise or dilute your voice, but may require some amplification, depending on the size of audiences you are addressing.

If you are speaking to a group with less than 40 people, I would suggest that you don't bother with amplification. Unless you have an awful room or are in an outdoor setting, your audience should be able to hear you at your normal tone of voice without too much effort. Except when you find yourself at a venue where you're competing with other noise (and I have seen many networking events held in pubs that fall into this category), you shouldn't need a microphone. Even if you have a quiet voice, speaking without a microphone creates a more intimate experience for your audience. Don't worry, they will lean in to hear you.

Once you get beyond that number, however, it will become increasingly difficult for your audience to catch your every word without using a microphone and some type of sound system.

TYPES OF MICROPHONES

CLIP-ON MICS

If you are using a microphone, lapel-type microphones, usually called lavalieres, are to be preferred over hand-held microphones, as they leave your hands free to invite your audience into your presentation and to add meaning to your words. But if you're behind a lectern or podium, you could be faced with a fixed microphone.

FIXED MICS

If this is the case, you'll necessarily be restricted in your movements. But do try to have the amplification set to a level sufficient for you to stand back a little from the podium, so you can be easily seen rather than being somewhat hidden. You wouldn't have a conversation with others while obscured by a pillar or any other object, so don't do this just because you're having a one-to-many conversation.

HAND-HELD MICS

Lastly, there's the much more common hand-held microphone, which creates another dilemma. What do you do with your hands now? You clearly need to use one hand to hold the microphone, which leaves you just one free hand for gesturing. But what happens if you need access to notes, or you're using slides and need to move these on? Speaking without access to notes is a step too far for most ordinary mortals, if you're expected to speak for quite a while.

Truth be told, this can be quite an issue, and it's one commonly and sometimes even mindlessly ignored by those who organise events (or sometimes, even by the speakers themselves)! This calls for planning. Where and how can you access notes with relative ease, with the least possible interruption to your flow, and without having to regularly disconnect from your audience?

Outside of using PowerPoint to share your speaking notes, which is a terrible idea and I'll explain why later, the four most common means of tacking this issue are:

1. Standing behind a lectern or podium

2. Placing notes on a table or a stool

3. Holding notes in your free hand

4. Trying to get through the speech without notes

Of these, never try to do the latter unless you've been speaking about your topic for a very long time, maybe even years. If what you want to say is so ingrained that you can hold court about it without straining your memory, fine, you go right ahead. But that's a big ask for almost everyone else. So what about the other options?

Standing behind the podium is the least risky approach for a speaker. But you'll often find yourself expected to speak with just a microphone and no podium available. In this case, do yourself a favour and contact the event organiser in advance and ask what the set-up is going to be and check the microphone and podium situation. That way you can feel more comfortable and do a better job for your audience.

Let the organisers know what you need, so you know beforehand where you will be able to stand and where you can place and access your notes. Then make it a habit to get to your venue early, to check that everything is as you expect. If it's not, at least you'll have enough time to do something about it. See chapter 19 for more about last minute checks and logistics.

CHAPTER FIFTEEN

TIME MANAGEMENT

"When a sermon at length comes to an end, people rise and praise God, and they feel the same way after many other speeches!"

John Andrew Holmes

ACHIEVING GOOD TIME MANAGEMENT

Let's talk about time. Consider time to be a fundamental parameter or constraint within which you need to work. One of the most important things you need to do before writing a speech is to find out just how much time you have to speak for.

The last thing you want to do is to try to cram too much material into too short a space of time. A lesser sin is to turn up at an event where you're expected to speak for say 40 minutes or an hour, and only have a speech that will take a fraction of that time to deliver.

Speakers who hog the podium for too long are the bane of every event organiser. By speaking for longer than they should, they run the risk of boring audiences, potentially messing up the impact other speakers could have by curtailing their time, wrecking catering arrangements, eating into precious networking time, and more.

This scourge happens in events large and small. In this extract from a 2012 article called 'Keep Talking' by LP from The Economist, you'll get a sense of how bad things can get in even the most high profile of events...

Verbosity at the UN: Keep talking

Fewer dictators means better timekeeping at the UN General Assembly... UN protocol since 2003 stipulates that heads of state addressing the General Assembly must keep within a 15-minute limit. Barack Obama has breached that every year of his presidency with orations of at least 30 minutes. But modern efforts pall against the giants of the past. Cuba's Fidel Castro in 1960 gave the longest ever continuous speech to the General Assembly, a fatiguing four hours and 29 minutes.

But the lengthiest speech ever at the UN (to the Security Council, not the General Assembly) was in 1957, when India's representative, VK Krishna Menon, outlined in some detail India's stand on Kashmir. It took eight hours, spread over three sessions, after which he collapsed.

Source: 'Verbosity at the UN: Keep Talking', LP, The Economist, 26 September 2012

I'm not surprised he collapsed! Is it possible he was deluded enough to think anyone was interested or listening to him? Not only do speakers virtually guarantee irritation by being long-winded, but they are setting their audience up for an unpleasant experience and the near certainty that the latter won't remember much of anything said!

FIT YOUR WORDS TO THE TIME SLOT

Once you know what time is available to you, and you write a speech to fit comfortably within this, you need to test your use of time:

- Time your speech as you practise out loud.
- Allow what you believe will be enough time for any interaction you need or wish to encourage.

SPEED CONTROLS

Having done this, you now need to allow for the rule of 25 per cent when speaking in public. In a live environment, you're likely to find your speech will take more time to deliver than when you practise it out loud – by about a quarter. How come?

This is because things happen in a live situation that don't occur when you're limbering up in private. There's interaction, audience movement, extra things that occur to you while giving the speech that you didn't think of when preparing, and you now find yourself mentioning these examples and anecdotes, etc.

It's important that you give yourself extra time to allow for these things, even if they don't all happen, as it will avoid you either speeding up or editing out chunks of your speech. Supposing you have 20 minutes to speak, and the practised aloud version of your speech runs for 20 minutes. What happens if there is more interaction, or there are distractions that cause more time to be used up earlier in your speech than you expected? In most cases, speakers will tend to speed up, and if you do this you'll face a few issues:

- You'll make it more difficult for your audience to keep up with you.

- You may start to feel and look more stressed, as you worry about how you're going to finish on time.

- You may feel you now have to drop parts of your speech altogether, which could result in you giving less of a presentation than planned.

ADVANTAGES OF USING LESS TIME AVAILABLE

The solution is to not put yourself under such pressure in the first place. By ensuring that your speech runs to no more than 75 per cent of the time available to you, you will be better off immediately because:

- **You'll take the heat off.**

  You won't feel under pressure to drop much of your material if you're no longer anxious regarding time.

- **Your audience is more likely to hear everything.**

  Audiences struggle to hear sentences that run into each other and are delivered at breakneck speed!

- **You won't appear panicked.**

  Be aware that audiences commonly perceive speakers who speak too fast as nervous or anxious (often correctly), and if they sense a speaker is uncomfortable, they'll tend to feel the same way. This has the potential to have an audience paying more attention to your disposition than what you want to share with them. Never a good plan.

···

- **You'll look good!**

  There's another bonus. You'll be popular with event organisers, because you make their lives easier when they don't have to juggle time around speakers who just can't stick to agreed timeframes. You'll either finish in good time or even a little bit earlier, and this can be a good thing. Remember, speakers are never shot by audiences for finishing early...

Apply the rule of 25% to your practiced out loud speech to allow for extra time you'll commonly need when speaking live.

CHAPTER SIXTEEN

CONSIDERING THE VENUE AND MEANS OF DELIVERY

"Politics is the art of controlling your environment."

Hunter S. Thompson

16

AUDIENCE LAYOUT

The layout of the audience may also have a bearing on your delivery and interaction. You might not have any option, but often you may be asked if there is a particular layout you'd like or have the chance to request one. Here are the most popular styles and some thoughts on when and why each may be suitable or not for what you want to achieve.

THEATRE STYLE

This is the most common format, where chairs are in rows and columns. If this is your preferred layout and you want to interact with your audience by getting among them, be sure to ask for aisles to make this possible.

A big pro for this format is that it's easier for you to cause cascade effects with your audience, where they will reflect back your nods, smiles or laughs as well as those they see around them. A con is that you typically make it more difficult for your audience to take many notes when you use this format. So if you're planning on giving a lecture of sorts and people need to jot things down, then maybe you need a different arrangement.

CLASSROOM STYLE

This is as it sounds. You use a collection of desks, long tables or chairs with a small table where attendees can write with ease. The biggest snag with this arrangement is that you are going to be less connected with your audience when you use it. They have desks between you and them, and you're encouraging them to behave like students, taking notes and therefore not looking at you the whole time you're speaking.

You're also making it easier for modern audience members to fire up laptops and mobile phones, and they can use them and not listen to you, or only partially pay attention. As you may have gathered, I'm not a big fan of this format; however, if you need your audience to pay attention to precise details and they absolutely should take notes, then go ahead.

HORSESHOE STYLE

This can be quite a good format when you want to create a mini-amphitheatre, where everyone is looking at you. It's also quite good for cascade effects. It's a more intimate format and is perhaps best suited to eight to 20 people in attendance. Any more than that and it doesn't work; any less and you don't benefit from it. If you use this format for more than 20 people you'll find it gets a bit unwieldy, and you'll struggle to achieve a level of intimacy that is possible with smaller numbers.

 Always consider the layout of your audience when planning your delivery and interaction.

ROUND TABLE

While this is sometimes used for larger groups, I recommend that you only consider this format for smaller meetings or break-out sessions, where you can fit your audience or a team around a table. This has the benefits of making sure everyone can see each other and encouraging plenty of interaction.

As you can imagine, if you use this set-up for larger groups and hence use many tables, too many people will find themselves with their backs to you or having to sit side-on to you. Apart from the fact that this can be a tad uncomfortable, it also reduces the cascade effects that you can achieve with a theatre style.

PREVIEW THE ROOM

If an event is important enough to you and it's possible, take the time to familiarise yourself with the venue where you will speak.

- Where will people be sitting?
- What is the layout of the room?
- Where will you be, relative to your audience?
- If you need somewhere to put notes while you speak, where can you put these?
- What happens if there's no podium or lectern, and you have to rely on putting your notes down on a low-slung table? Will you be able to read your notes from there?
- If not, can you find a better piece of furniture you can use?

See chapter 19 for more about logistics on the day.

CHAPTER SEVENTEEN

YOUR APPEARANCE

"Clothes make the man. Naked people have little or no influence on society."

Mark Twain

17

FIRST IMPRESSIONS MATTER

Do first impressions count? Do audiences really care about your appearance and whether you're dressed up or positively dressed down? This is a surprisingly common question at our seminars and I always give the same tongue-in-cheek answer: 'To a fashion!' Now before you groan, let me explain.

Appearances matter. Even if you think audiences shouldn't judge a book by its cover, they will. In the same way that most of us instinctively size people and situations up all the time, audiences are no different and will often make judgments about speakers before they say a word. They make decisions regarding what they think you might have to say and how they should regard you within moments of seeing you, as they listen to introductions.

This is a make or break time for all speakers, when people decide if you're someone that's worth paying attention to. Commonly these assessments are based on nothing more than gut reactions. Appearances therefore count.

These assessments can colour their attitudes to speakers at many levels, influencing the level of authority, credibility, likeability and friendliness they associate with those who are due to speak. Of course, this doesn't mean that speakers can't turn these attitudes around through their content and delivery, but it affects the point from which they start.

WHAT YOUR CLOTHES SAY ABOUT YOU

In a fascinating review of recent research on this topic by Margaret Stuntz-Tresky, findings from myriad studies established that audiences tend to accord greater credibility and trust to speakers who are perceived to be better or more formally dressed.

In study after study, those who were considered to be more casually dressed were deemed to be a weaker source of information than more formally dressed providers of exactly the same information or instructions. More formally addressed speakers were considered more expert and trustworthy, and they also achieved far greater compliance with their requests, even when these were quite unreasonable!

Perhaps surprisingly in this age of equality, it appears that attire is given a greater importance in the level of authority and expertise associated with a female speaker than with male counterparts.

Appearances matter. Even if you think audiences shouldn't judge a book by its cover, they will.

Authority effect of clothes

In his bestselling book *Influence: The Psychology of Persuasion*, **Dr. Robert Cialdini** spoke about the authority effect of clothes and how they can influence our willingness to comply with requests from others.

In addition to citing 'man on the street' tests run by psychologist Leonard Bickman, which proved the average citizen was hugely more likely to comply with odd requests made by a man wearing a uniform than if the same man was wearing ordinary clothes; he told a great story about research done in Texas regarding another form of uniform – a well-tailored business suit.

In this study it was arranged that a 31-year-old man would violate the law by crossing the street against the traffic laws on a variety of occasions. In half of the cases, he was dressed in a freshly pressed business suit and tie; on the other occasions, he wore a work shirt and trousers.

The researchers then watched to see what people would do. Who would follow him? And guess what? Three and a half times more people followed the 'suited jaywalker' as against when he was less smartly attired.

And this effect spills over into the office and even the sales room. Those who dress better are more highly trusted and persuasive.

So what does this mean to you? While I will limit the amount of fashion advice in this book, the moral of the story is that paying attention to how you dress and your grooming can make a difference to the type of reception you receive from your target audiences. In general, it's probably better to be dressed smartly at all times.

TIPS TO ALWAYS LOOK THE PART

Fashion adviser Ruth Murphy offers a number of suggestions on appearances that you may find helpful.

TIPS FOR MEN AND WOMEN

1. Pay attention to grooming: if your hair or nails look scruffy or unkempt, your audience may conclude that you don't pay attention to detail.

2. Although it's rumoured to be an ancient art now, practised in just a few remote parts of the globe, polish your shoes. You can ruin the effect of a superb outfit by having shoes that fail to complement your look.

3. Make sure your clothes fit you: it's astonishing how many speakers fail to notice that parts of their outfits are too tight. This tends to make the speaker look uncomfortable and, while your audience may feel for you on this front, it can be distracting and should be avoided.

4. If in doubt, it's better to be overdressed for a speaking engagement than the opposite. People will see you've made the effort and you can often lose a tie or accessory if your audience is more casually attired than you.

FOR MEN

1. If wearing a suit, most men look better in darker suits, providing you don't look like a judge or undertaker. Many people believe that navy suits, in particular, engender more trust. However, dark grey or black suits – with or without faint stripes – can also be just the ticket.

2. If you have a pale complexion, try to steer away from pure white shirts. They can make you look like death warmed up!

3. If you have a ruddy, sallow or dark complexion, a crisp white shirt can look spectacular.

4. Use ties to add personality. Try to choose a tie with a bit of colour, as this suggests someone who is likely to be more engaging. Remember, red is often considered a power colour but not everyone feels comfortable wearing it.

5. Tie your tie properly: a badly done tie or one that doesn't cover your top button looks just as scruffy as unkempt hair. So take a few moments to make sure you finish the look you were after.

FOR WOMEN

1. Remember that fit and colours are more important than almost everything else. They give you more authority and will help you feel more confident.

2. Avoid clothes that look overly masculine. For instance, wearing a suit that looks boxy can make a woman appear much bigger than she is.

3. As Lilly Walters, a US communications specialist, once put it, 'the higher the neckline the less frivolous you appear'.

4. Don't button jackets.

5. Don't go overboard with clunky jewellery: it's better to go simple or unfussy.

6. Do use scarves to add personality to an outfit. It's a bit like ties for men.

7. For women with pale complexions, in addition to avoiding white shirts or blouses that make you look drained of energy, steer clear of rose and cool tones for the same reason.

CHAPTER EIGHTEEN

GAINING ATTENTION BEFORE YOU SAY A WORD

"You never get a second chance to make a first impression."

Mark Twain

THE ROLE OF INTRODUCTIONS

Now we come to a part of presenting that is too often forgotten. You've worked hard on your audience analysis, message development, speech preparation and practice, and now you're good to go. Hold your horses! You may have forgotten something...

Your introduction can often be the first thing that people get to hear about you. It tells people something about who you are and what they can expect. That much is obvious. But what may not be so obvious is how critical a role your introduction plays in how people perceive you before you get started.

If you are announced to an audience in a dull, uninspired or even downright poor fashion, make no mistake, this will make an impression on your audience, and not a good one. If your audience starts off with a view that you're probably not worth listening to (and bear in mind, you haven't started yet), you now have anything from a hill to a mountain to climb.

Audiences make snap decisions about speakers all the time, especially when they have to listen to more than one speaker. They make calls on who is worthy of their time and who they may choose to drown out. It's not because they're being miserable, they're just filtering, in the same way you filter information that comes your way every day.

Be in no doubt, done correctly, an introduction can help your audience form the view that they should pay attention and that you are someone who is likely to be interesting and credible.

> ## Never leave your introduction to chance. Always write your own.

MAKE YOUR OWN ANNOUNCEMENT

Find out in advance who will be introducing you. And understand that just because someone is expected to announce different speakers, it doesn't mean that they have to announce everyone or everything. If may be possible to announce yourself, so do ask. In any case, it's always a good idea to decide beforehand what you would be happy to have an announcer say, and what you may want to say yourself. Sometimes you're better off simply asking the MC to just say something like:

> 'And now I would like to introduce [your name], who will tell you about himself/herself.'

After all, when it comes to introductions, who is better to introduce you than yourself?

Bear in mind that people who are asked to introduce speakers commonly do so simply because they're there, and not because they are either qualified or chomping at the bit to do so. Therefore, making their lives a little easier will usually be appreciated. That said, in the same way that you must always assess your audience, know who you're dealing with when it comes to likely announcers. If they're great speakers and well-regarded, they can boost your credibility. It's up to you which technique you adopt, but don't leave your introductions to chance.

PRESSURE TO MAKE A RETORT

Another incentive for making your own introduction is that you may have little or no control over what the announcer will say. So much so that you might be taken by surprise by his or her comments and unable to respond appropriately. The last thing you need is pressure to make a suitable riposte, as seen in the following example.

Pressure to respond

Comedic actor Tim Allen had every reason to be furious about the way he was introduced as a presenter at the Golden Globes in 2011. Many felt the host for the event, Ricky Gervais, went past gentle ribbing and was downright offensive in the way he paved the way for Tom Hanks and Tim Allen to present an award. Here's what he said:

'Okay, what can I say about our next two presenters?

'The first is an actor, producer, writer and director, whose movies have grossed over $3.5 billion at the box office. He's won two Academy Awards and three Golden Globes for his powerful and varied performances, starring in such films as Philadelphia, Forrest Gump, Cast Away, Apollo 13 and Saving Private Ryan.

'The other,' he continued, while flipping his notes backwards and forwards at a loss for something to say, '... is Tim Allen!'

Perhaps not surprisingly, you could see Tom and Tim (and the audience) take a deep intake of breath before the duo tried to come up with a few on-the-spot, witty ripostes.

This is a great example of why trying to think up a retort on the spot is difficult and unlikely to be very successful. Now, while it's not very likely you will have people announcing you looking for cheap laughs, I've lost count of the number of times I've seen an MC or compère mess things up for a speaker by:

- Boring everyone silly by making, or worse still, reading an introduction that goes on and on and on. And, in the process, a less experienced or polished MC will often fail to tell the audience what the talk will be about and/or why they should listen, as they don't realise this is their job.

- Making cringe worthy mistakes about the speaker's credentials or the topic at hand.

- Conjuring things up out of the air. (This happens more often than you might think, especially if the speaker hasn't armed the MC with something to say.)

- Summing up what the speaker plans to say before a word is said, leaving the audience to wonder why they should bother to listen to the speaker at all now (and the speaker may be thinking just the same).

The moral of the story is this: don't leave this job to chance.

SET GOALS

What goals should you set for your introduction? How much can you do with it? Here are three ideas that will help. Use introductions to tell your audience:

1. Who you are.
2. Why they should listen to you. This should be no more than a few sentences that speak to your knowledge or experience and will encourage your audience to believe you're likely to know what you're talking about and have insights worth sharing.
3. What you want to talk to the audience about (what's in it for them).

You don't need your introduction to steal your thunder. Rather, think of it as an advertisement for what will follow. Here's an example. If you're planning to speak to an audience about how they could fix a problem they care about, you might ask for the following introduction:

··

'At a time when ABC is happening, resulting in DEF [a central problem] – XYZ [speaker's name] is going to address you on ways we might tackle these issues.'

··

Be brief. There is no need for a lengthy introduction. The longer it is the less people will absorb. Audiences only use introductions to make decisions about whether they should hit their 'on' or 'off' buttons.

THE USE OF BIOS

Many event organisers seek biographies (bios) from speakers before events, and they will tend to include these in marketing literature beforehand as well as in their 'on-the-day' packs or folders. Check whether this is the case.

If there are two sets of information, as noted above, use your bios and your introductions in two different ways for more attention and impact. You can include more detailed and general information about who you are and what you have achieved in the former, together with some indication of what you will speak about, focusing on the headline, as this is what people will pay attention to if deciding whether to choose your session versus another.

Then use your introduction in a more personalised fashion, maybe even including a story about why you're likely to interest your audience in the on-the-day material.

CHAPTER NINETEEN

LAST MINUTE CHECKS

"Trust, but verify."

Ronald Reagan

Almost wrapping up time? Not quite. By now, we've busted many a myth and you should have a good understanding of what is required to develop core public speaking skills. Now you have to plan your logistics.

PLANNING YOUR LOGISTICS

ARRIVE IN GOOD TIME

In addition to allowing 25 per cent extra time on your practised aloud speech, make sure you also allow yourself plenty of time before you step up to the podium. Don't ever rock up to a presentation with just moments to go. Even if you're not the sort to be nervous before speaking, I encourage you to get to the venue where you will speak at least 30 minutes before your due time. If you're one of a series of speakers, work to a similar amount of time before the first of these is due to speak.

EXPECT THE UNEXPECTED

Allow for the litany of things that can cause anyone to be late getting to your speaking engagement, everything from issues with finding your venue to transport problems and even locating the room in which you're due to appear. See also chapter 20 for more about dealing with the unexpected.

CHECK THE EQUIPMENT – ALLOW FOR MURPHY'S LAW

Once you've found the room where you'll speak, make sure you have enough time to confirm any equipment you need is both there and in working order. It is extraordinary how frequently technical issues can delay or even derail presentations.

Interestingly, the biggest source of problems is invariably not the sound systems or dodgy microphones, it's PowerPoint. Far too many speakers encounter issues with getting projectors to work, connecting PCs to projectors or a basic inability to open their PowerPoint files. Why put yourself under this pressure? It can wreck the cool of even the most seasoned of campaigners. Arrive early, ensure any kit you need is working, and then relax and mingle.

See chapter 20 for a more thorough look at this issue.

MAKE CONTACTS AND CONNECTIONS

There's another advantage to getting there early. In almost all circumstances, you'll find some other people will also arrive early, just as others could manage to be late for their own funerals! It's their nature and meeting with those early birds is a golden opportunity for a worm like you.

Before proceedings get under way, try to engage these people in some light chat, maybe asking them something about themselves, why they're at the event or what they're hoping to get out of it. Make your chat all about the other people and what matters to them – not about you. Not surprisingly, most of us like to have others express interest in us, so you're now well on your way to making sure that before you start speaking, you'll already have some extra friends or people well disposed towards you in your audience.

This is wonderful, as you'll find it easier to include these people in your audience eye contact while you speak. You can nod or smile at them, and, in most cases, they will be paying rapt attention to you – just as you did to them before the 'off'. So if you nod imperceptibly or smile from time to time, they are likely to reflect this behaviour. Then the people beside them will be hard-pressed not to follow suit. We all tend to mirror and reflect back the body language we see around us whenever we are in company.

In essence, by arriving early, you're creating a nice supportive group of 'nodder' allies. And as a speaker, you love these guys. They're mood setters.

PRE-PRESENTATION CHECKLIST

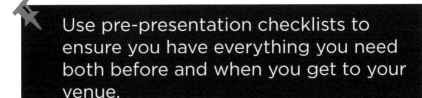

Use pre-presentation checklists to ensure you have everything you need both before and when you get to your venue.

Here is your pre-presentation checklist by way of a final check or aide-mémoire. By now your homework in terms of your speech should be done.

- **Homework done?**

  o ARC (Audience analysis, relevance and credibility)

  o What you want to say; preparation

  o Practice

- **Lists**

  Think like a scout leader. Create a list of everything you need to bring and check before you leave home. Then make a second checklist of things to check on the day.

- **Seating**

  Pre-plan and prearrange your preferred seating arrangements. Ask for a seating arrangement that will suit your style of speaking and the type of interaction you feel you need to accomplish what you are setting out to do with your audience.

- **Microphones**

  Choose your weapons wisely, if you have a choice. If not, find out what you are up against. Your preferred option should be to seek a lavalier, the small, attachable microphone. Make sure you check your equipment is working long before you need to use it.

- **Location**

  Where do you stand? Podium, lectern, table or nuttin? This depends on you and the level of interaction you want to achieve with your audience, as well as the set-up you are presented with.

- **Continuous improvement**

  At every juncture, ask yourself 'what will create a better experience for the audience?' as well as 'how do I feel?' You want your audience to see and hear you at your most relaxed and engaging.

Don't give out copies of your presentation in advance of when you speak.

ON-THE-DAY CHECKLIST

- **Arrival:** Arrive sufficiently early that you can run through your checklist of things you want to check, and also have enough time to fix any problems before you speak.

- **Microphones:** Are your microphones working? Are there any back-up options if anything goes wrong while you speak?

- **Sound check:** Do a sound check in advance of having your audience in place if possible.

- **Equipment:** If you're using slides or videos, connect your laptop or the computer made available to you to the projector (or make sure this has been done), access your presentation file and make sure it's correctly loaded and projecting as you expect.

- **Size of venue:** Be aware that different venues will have different set-ups and the size of projection can have quite a bearing on what your audience sees.

- **Location:** Check out where you will stand and where you can put your notes. Can your audience see you easily, or do you need to stand to the side or in front of any lectern or podium made available to you?

- **Space requirements:** Beware the space required for laptops and microphones can often reduce or eliminate space you may need to access notes. Using small 6 by 4 inch postcards with bullet points is helpful, as they require very little space.

- **Notes table:** If you don't have anywhere to put notes, ask for a small table that is high enough to place your notes on.

- **Stowing equipment:** Where can you stow any equipment you bring to a speaking event securely when not speaking or networking?

- **Meet and greet:** Once you're happy that your equipment and event set-up are in good order, be sure to meet, greet and speak with any announcer who may introduce you and those organising the event you're attending. The announcer is especially important in order to finalise, if you haven't already done so, who will say what and when.

- **Handouts and other audience materials:** Check you have sufficient materials to give the audience? Can these be left on an after-event table for easy access?

- **Materials and props:** Anything required during your session must be in place, for example, paper, pens, props, images, etc.

CHAPTER TWENTY

DEALING WITH THE UNEXPECTED

"Some things are so unexpected that no one is prepared for them."

Leo Rosten

20

No matter how well you prepare, no matter how committed you are to the craft of being the best speaker you can be, no matter what steps you take to avoid common snafus with equipment or room set-ups, stuff can still go wrong. Equipment can fail, interruptions can stem a speech in full flow, a point or story you felt sure your audience would lap up can fall flat! So what do you do when things go awry? There are a number of answers to this situation.

ALWAYS HAVE BACK-UP PLANS

First, have back-up plans for common problems. What happens if you're mid-stream in your speech and something happens that could distract or even derail you? An alarm goes off, someone's mobile phone rings, the laptop dies, the podium disengages from the stage, your microphone goes dead, etc. Do feel free to add in your own bad experiences or worst nightmares. These can and do happen on occasion.

TECHNICAL HITCHES: POWERPOINT OR SLIDES

- Bring your own laptop with the files you need, just in case the event organiser's kit doesn't work.

- Copy your file onto a memory stick and bring it as a spare.
- Email yourself a copy of the file to an email service you can readily access from the internet, if needs be.
- Print off a hard copy of your slides in case all else fails.

My wife features in a good example of how things can go wrong when relying on PowerPoint, even when you take extra precautions.

Being overly reliant on slides

My wife had just been appointed the national coordinator for a environmental awareness group in Dublin, and was asked to give a talk at an offline event for large online networking communities for Irish small- and medium-sized enterprises.

Although an inexperienced speaker, she agreed to speak and dutifully created a PowerPoint deck to cover the main points she wanted to share on the day. Then, for good measure and to ward against things that might go wrong, she:

- Copied the presentation to her desktop, for easy access if using her own laptop at the event.

- Created an extra version of her slides in a previous version of PowerPoint, on the off-chance she might need to use someone else's computer and they didn't have the latest version of PowerPoint installed.

- Copied the presentation to a USB memory stick in case she ran into any snags using her own PC or anyone else's.

- Sent herself a copy of the same file on email in case anything else could go wrong with any of the above.

So that was all very sensible. However, despite all these efforts, she found out on the day that she had completely wasted her time. It turned out that the venue for the event was a beautifully converted annex to an old stately home in Ireland. And while it had a small stage and great lighting, it had no projectors and no possible surface against which a PowerPoint presentation might be used.

Fortunately, my wife was able to make light of the situation and refer from time to time to one more piece of back-up she had put in place. She had also printed out her slides and was able to say to her audience, with a good deal of self-deprecation and exaggeration, on a number of occasions:

'Now, if you could only see this slide, you'd see...'

So, while she coped with this experience though improvisation, there's a moral to this story: don't get caught out by being overly reliant on slides. While it's perfectly okay to use them for effect, it's a good idea to figure out in advance how you would function if you had to work without them. The last thing you need is to be thrown off-guard and unable to share your words as you wish.

Even if you don't need to rely on any of these back-up plans, knowing that you can will help to calm nerves. You're ready if stuff won't work or you need to improvise.

UPSIDE TO MALFUNCTIONS

If, after all that, the projector at your event isn't working or you find there's no way to get a laptop connected to the blasted thing, you're still more than okay, because although your audience won't be able to see your slides at the time, you can use the lack of slides as a reason why your audience should share email details with you to get a copy of your slides later. In addition, the slides shouldn't be as big a deal if these were there purely to amplify the points you want to make.

This could actually be a blessing in disguise, as most people don't bother to re-read copies of slides they receive at an event. But now you'll have an opportunity to reinforce the arguments you make for your audience and to create further calls to action via communications that will almost assuredly be read. Guess what, they might even be shared with others. Wouldn't that be cool? You've just gone viral!

SOUND MALFUNCTIONS

After laptop and projector problems, sound issues come in a close second for stuff that malfunctions. Knowing that, always ask in advance what back-up arrangement are available for microphones, so you know what to do when one goes dead, instead of looking confused. More often than not, event locations will have extra microphones and/or batteries on hand to fix the situation.

DISTRACTIONS

Ask your 'what if 'questions in advance. A little bit of pre-emptive thinking can be all it takes to solve problems before they occur. If you encounter other distractions, such as alarms going off, noise from adjoining rooms, things falling (whether you've knocked them to the floor or not), don't panic. See if you can just make light of it, or maybe even integrate it into your presentation.

For instance, if you hear sirens as you speak, you could say something like:

> 'I guess the word is out that I'm going to spill the beans about XXX – I'm in trouble now!'

Of course, you shouldn't try to overly milk the situation and feel you need to be the king or queen of improv, coining a perfect and amusing response to whatever just happened.

Rather, you are merely showing your audience that you are relaxed and want to reassure them you are focused on them and their experience.

MOBILE PHONES

These days it's all too common for speeches to be interrupted by a mobile phone going off. How you choose to handle this is very much a matter of personal style.

You can use it as an opportunity to ask others to turn theirs off. For instance, I quite like the following gentle, and usually well-received approach before a speech begins:

> 'Would you please remember to turn on your mobile phones...Just as soon as this presentation is over?'

Equally, you can make light of it, saying something like:

> 'Oh, that'll be for me...'

But whatever you do, don't get annoyed at the apparent lack of consideration or respect. It'll show, and that's never a good thing.

LOSING YOUR TRAIN OF THOUGHT

Naturally, losing your train of thought is something that can cause major embarrassment. If you lose your place, think like a news anchor that's in the middle of a bulletin when a technical issue means a clip or interview with a reporter can't be introduced. Faced with this snag, most newscasters will acknowledge the problem, promise to come back to the issue later (if this is possible), pause for a few seconds and then move on to what's next.

As a speaker you can adopt a fairly similar approach. Acknowledge that there was something else you wanted to say on whatever the topic was, suggest you'll come back to it if it comes back to you, pause to find your place in your notes, look up at your audience and move on to what you wanted to say next.

Audiences are far more forgiving than many speakers think. Few people expect perfection and you may even find many people won't even notice what you perceived to be a hole in your presentation.

UNEXPECTED QUESTIONS

Unforeseen questions and comments or a poor Q&A session can throw you, especially if you are unprepared. See chapter 10 for more on handling questions and comments.

Be prepared. Always have back up plans for common problems both before and even while you're speaking.

CONCLUSION

Remember, everything you do when speaking to an audience is about them and their experiences, it's never about you.

I wish you every success and hope you have as much benefit from learning the art of public speaking as many of my Reluctant Speakers' Club members have over the years. This vital skill can truly make the difference to your profile, your business and your confidence.

Oh, and one more thing, always remember – it's fun.

NEXT STEPS

This step-by-step guide to creating inspiring and memorable talks was written to share with you exactly what it takes to overcome anxieties you may have about public speaking and to create, hone and deliver a great speech. The key now is this. The more you follow the steps in the book, the faster you'll become a more confident and persuasive speaker.

And to help you to put these tools, techniques and ideas into practice, be sure to register for free bonus materials available to you on **www.howtomakepowerfulspeeches.com**

When you visit this resource page, you'll find speech writing templates, articles, podcast interviews, videos and other bonus materials.

I look forward to seeing you there.

ENJOYED THIS BOOK?

If you've enjoyed this book and found it helpful, I would be delighted if you'd consider leaving a review at Amazon to say so.

Just as positive word-of-mouth can boost the impact of your speeches after you've stepped away from the podium, your recommendation on Amazon can make a world of difference and would be very much appreciated.

GET IN TOUCH

To get Eamonn's latest articles and podcasts, please visit:

http://www.thereluctantspeakersclub.com/blog/

Eamonn speaks frequently on how to inspire others through public speaking and how to captivate any audience through storytelling. He delivers keynote addresses, master classes and workshops on these topics that can be tailored to your needs. If you would like to find out more, please email: **eobrien@thersc.ie**

You can also connect with Eamonn on

Twitter (at **@thereluctantsc**) and

Google Plus (at **https://www.google.com/+EamonnOBrien**)

ABOUT THE AUTHOR

In his book 'How to make Powerful Speeches' and through his experiences as founder of the Reluctant Speakers Club; Eamonn can help you to banish your fears of the podium forever.

In addition to being the CEO of The Reluctant Speakers Club, Eamonn is also the President of Professional Speaking Association Ireland and the author of the award winning The Reluctant Speakers Club blog and podcasts. And his podcast is included in the current Top 100 Small Business Podcasts by Small Biz Trends.

Eamonn works with senior executives and professionals to conquer fears of speaking in public with confidence. Members learn how to hone their communication skills and speak with an unprecedented degree of clarity, persuasiveness and authority.

Over his 25 plus years in senior international sales and marketing roles, Eamonn O'Brien has run countless training courses on developing communication skills in the USA and in Ireland. He is a frequent speaker at international marketing events in North America, the UK, France, and other European countries.

He holds an MBA from Manchester Business School and a BSc (Management) from Trinity College Dublin. He has also been a long time member of ESOMAR, the world association of market research professionals.

As a marketing consultant, he has worked with many international companies including AT&T, Johnson & Johnson, Capital One, Citibank, Harvard Business Review, and the Smithsonian.

24565290R00132

Made in the USA
San Bernardino, CA
29 September 2015